COURAGE TO BE MYSELF

COURAGE TO BE MYSELF

Carlos G. Valles, S.J.

DOUBLEDAY

NEW YORK LONDON TORONTO SYDNEY AUCKLAND

PUBLISHED BY DOUBLEDAY
A division of Bantam Doubleday Dell Publishing Group, Inc.
666 Fifth Avenue, New York, New York 10103

DOUBLEDAY and the portrayal of an anchor with a dolphin
are trademarks of Doubleday, a division of Bantam Doubleday
Dell Publishing Group, Inc.

Library of Congress Cataloging-in-Publication Data

Vālesa, Father, 1925–
Courage to be myself / Carlos G. Valles.
    p.   cm.
  ISBN 0-385-26383-X
  1. Spiritual life—Catholic authors.
2. Identification (Religion)
I.   Title.
BX2350.2.V17   1989   89-30934
248.4′82—dc19   CIP

For Maria,
who is praying for my conversion,
and Adela,
who has given up.

Contents

III   LIVING THE PRESENT

Maybe I lived the life of others.

Pablo Neruda.

I

OWNING
THE
PAST

1

Second-Hand People

The phrase hit me like a bullet. The book was still in my hands, but I had ceased to see the page, and only that sentence stood out bold and clear like a flash of lightning that reduces to mere background the whole black horizon. Sometimes a thought is in the mind seeking expression, and comes to life as it finds flesh and body in the sudden incarnation of exact language. Sometimes, on the contrary, the mind is utterly unprepared, oblivious or even defensive, and the unexpected revelation of the printed challenge uncovers a new world of creative adventure. Such was the case now. Smug complacency had led me to believe that I was a free and independent individual, fruit of my own thoughts and master of my own actions, and now suddenly I knew I was not. I felt unmasked by the unerring blow. The book had done its job. The sentence had struck home.

The book was written by J. Krishnamurti, and the sentence was: "We are second-hand people." I stopped reading. I slowly put the book down. I wouldn't read further. I was a second-hand person. I had been found out. What was worse, I had found out finally myself, and that was the crisis. I *am* second-hand.

I have always looked down on second-hand goods. The very fact that someone else has used them before makes them tainted, unreliable, polluted. "As good as new" claims the advertisement, only to emphasize the fact that it is not new. The second owner is deprived of the virgin pleasure of the first touch, the fresh look, the early perfume. He or she only uses what someone else has used before. Practical and cheap, but devoid of surprise and thrill. If I put on a second-hand sweater I cannot help thinking I am in someone else's frame, I have lost part of my personality by assuming a garment someone has used before. I prefer a new sweater, even of inferior quality, to a borrowed or inherited one even if the latter has brighter colors and richer design. Don't people pay special prices for the premiere of a film, for the first-day cover of a new postage stamp? My clothing is, in an external but true and definite way, part of me, and I want every part of me to be me.

And now I find out that it is not so. It is not only my sweater that is borrowed, but my thoughts, my principles, my tastes, and my convictions. It is not only my clothing, but my skin and bones as well. What I thought was exclusively and inalienably mine turns out to be commonplace inherited routine. I knew it deep down in the darkness of my unexpressed thoughts, but I had never wanted to admit it to myself. Only now when the bold indictment came from outside, the delayed revelation exploded into consciousness with all the contained fury of a mighty earthquake. I am not I. There is little of me in me. I am second-hand. What I call *my* ideas had all belonged to someone else. I have not thought them out by myself. My tastes are inherited, and if I had been born in a distant place with a different culture I would dislike things I relish now, and would relish things I now dislike. I am a bundle of prefabricated concepts. Even my reactions have been programmed by a careful training. What I call spontaneous in me is a well-rehearsed habit; what I consider genuine is only repeated artificiality. By dint of wearing these clothes I have come to believe that they were mine, but they all are second-hand, and the sudden discovery makes me feel uneasy in them.

Once I listened to a politician's well-prepared speech. He leaned heavily with careful intonation on the key words that preceded the policy statements after the inevitable platitudes: "I personally believe that . . . ," "It is my genuine conviction that . . . ," "I have arrived at the conclusion that. . . ." The words were those of personal idiom, but listening to them I knew that the politician was only broadcasting the party line. Tomorrow he may change allegiance and proclaim, with the same "conviction," that he genuinely believes in . . . exactly the contrary. What unsettles me now is to discover that I, too, have only been broadcasting the party line, while I told others, and had myself come to believe, that such was my personal conviction. Nice speech for an election campaign, but the pitiful reflection of an empty life. Most likely the politician's speech had been written for him by a shadow speech-writer. Will I let my life be only a speech written by someone else?

I know well that people cannot grow all by themselves. Rousseau's *Émile* is a utopia. A human child cannot be brought up without any influence, and indeed such an attempt would in itself be the worst and most crippling of all possible influences. A child has to be taught a language and a way of life, has to be trained in table manners and moral behavior. Nobody can build up his or her own life from scratch, nor, as an example, should I be expected to invent the decimal system by myself if I want to learn mathematics. I will do well to avail myself of the wisdom of mankind and of the textbooks that explain the development of mathematics up to the present day. The danger is that I may get stuck in the textbooks and contribute nothing original, nothing creative, nothing new to the knowledge and the experience that have gone before me. My life may become one more textbook, and textbooks are mostly copies from other textbooks, as people's lives are copies of other people's lives. We need personal research if mankind is to grow.

The awesome experiment was performed at least once by an inhuman hand. In the year 1828 there appeared in Nuremberg a man who had been chained in a cave shortly after his birth and had remained there in dark solitude for seventeen years. Food was brought to him while he was asleep, and he had seen no human being, had learned no language and acquired no culture. When unchained he was not able to walk, as he had not been trained to coordinate his reflexes and direct his muscles, and his eyes had the wild look of a demented brute. He was given the name of Kaspar Hauser, but his mystery was never solved. In fact, shortly after he was discovered, he was killed, probably by the same person who had confined him to the cave. A human being, to be a human being, needs help and training, has to be taught how to stand erect and how to take his first steps. He has to be given words and ideas, norms and values, has to learn how to look into other people's eyes and smile into their faces. A child brought up in a dark lonely cave becomes a monster, and the person who experiments with him, a criminal. Training is altogether necessary if a person is to become a person. Centuries of civilization have not passed in vain.

The danger is that since training is necessary it may become inviolable and sacrosanct. The hidden fallacy is in the subtle change from the fact that "some" training was necessary to the assumption that "this" training was the necessary and irreplaceable one, and so what was a mere accident of history becomes hallowed tradition. "This" is the right way, and "that" is not done. By you, of course. If the child had been born in another place he might have been taught Chinese instead of English, and in place of his five-o'clock tea he might be enjoying a cup of curdled cattle-blood on an African plain. He had to acquire some language and some eating habits, but the concrete habits as such are immaterial. In fact they condition him to a particular way of life which, however rewarding, is only one and thus limited. It is always enriching to learn a new language.

One important point must be made clear. When I wake up to the fact that I am a slave to my past, I am not quarreling with my past. Far from it. My past is fine, only in that it *is* past, and is not the ruler of my present. The foundations are fine as foundations, solid and steady in their underground firmness. But if I want to perpetuate the style and manner of the foundations in the rest of the building, I am going to come up with a rather bizarre structure. Now that I am aboveground, I want to design my own building and put doors and windows and towers and domes in it. I accept and welcome and am grateful for all the influences that have shaped my life; all that I want, now that I have come of age, is to take that life in my hands, and shape it from now on as I want it to be shaped. So far my past has owned me; now I want to own my past.

Another point. They also tell me that, though all the elements of my personality may be second-hand, the mixture which is me is unique, and that mixture is new and personal and individual. This also is very true, and, again, all that I now want is to be the one who determines the mixture, who decides from now on which elements in me, as I know myself now, are to remain in me as part of me, and which ones are to be shed so that I can control the mixture in proportions of my own liking. My morning starts from the moment I wake up (this in an Indian proverb). The canvas of my life has so far been painted over by foreign brushes. From now on I want to use my own brush.

For several years in my youth I studied under a man whose rigidity, asceticism, and unfailing sense of discipline made of him a ruthlessly efficient teaching machine. Many years later, with a change of job, place, and atmosphere, he became quite a different character—open, joyful, and charming, with a newly discovered personality. When people who had known him before (and had suffered under him before) said, "How much you have changed!" he would answer, "I have not changed. This is the way I always was down deep within myself, only that my true personality was suppressed and buried under layers of artificial self-control. Now I am at last the person I knew myself to be and was always meant to be." The sooner we make a similar discovery in our lives, the richer our lives will be.

This is Krishnamurti's quotation in full: "For centuries we have been spoon-fed by our teachers, by our authorities, by our books, our saints. We say, 'Tell me all about it—what lies beyond the hills and the mountains and the earth?' and we are satisfied with their descriptions, which means that we live on words and our life is shallow and empty. We are second-hand people. We have lived on what we have been told, either guided by our inclinations, our tendencies, or compelled to accept by circumstances and environment. We are the result of all kinds of influences and there is nothing new in us, nothing that we have discovered for ourselves; nothing original, pristine, clear. . . . To be free of all authority, of your own and that of another, is to die to everything of yesterday, so that your mind is always fresh, always young, innocent, full of vigour and passion." Freedom, in Borges' phrase, "from all the yesterdays of history."*

In Christian terms, translating into my own life and experience those words of wisdom, I think of death and resurrection in the mystery of our redemption. My own person, as I know myself now, is a fairly standard specimen of middle-class humanity. I could go on like this for the rest of my life, as most humans do, and add one more digit to the statistics of creation. But now that the angel of annunciation has winged his way through heavenly paths of divine providence and stood, gracious and challenging, on the threshold of my soul, I have the chance of breaking through a new incarnation of power and light, to die in my own image of mortal flesh in order to rise up in the splendor of the fullness of life that Jesus offers me. Death is painful because the old image, however drab and mediocre, was dear to me and I felt safe and comfortable in the familiarity of the borrowed clothes

* J. Krishnamurti, *Freedom from the Known*, edited by Mary Lutyens, Victor Gollanez, Ltd., 1977, pp. 10–19.

and the daily routine; but the nails and the cross are the only way to open the old tomb of custom and prejudice, and liberate the new person hidden in me and born anew in the early dawn of my own Easter Sunday. Paschal adventure in a new Promised Land.

2

My Own House to Live In

There is a regular conspiracy afoot not to let me be me. For my own good, of course, and with the best of intentions, but the plot has thickened throughout my life. The people who are closest to me and who love me most have been telling me since my tender years what I have to do and what I have to avoid, what I have to think and what I have to believe, what is right and what is wrong in this complicated world we live in. They have told me all this before I had a chance to figure it out by myself; and, not just telling me in words and commands which I could later recognize as such, and sift and accept or reject at will, they have also instilled into me all those rules of life and behavior without my realizing it, through custom and example, through penalties and rewards, through love and fear, till a whole code of conduct has been built up within me and into my system to preside over my actions for the rest of my life, and make me feel good when I conform to it, and guilty when I betray it.

I recognize the good will of those who shaped me, I admit the necessity of the process, I am grateful for the benefits I have derived from it—and now, at the dawn of a new awakening in my life, I want to survey the inner landscape of my soul, take it as it is, and get down to the challenging and exhilarating task of trying new designs and fixing new horizons for a new adventure in living.

Have you ever seen the light on the face of a man who is building his own house? For years he has lived in a rented house which someone else had built and in which other people had lived before, one tenant after another. He had furnished the house and decorated it to his own taste, to be sure, but the building was borrowed, the memories of other occupants hung heavy on the walls, the smell was ancient and the colors faded. And all along in his mind the dream of his own house had been taking shape. First as a pure fantasy, and then, little by little, as an increasingly approaching reality. He had designed it a thousand times in his imagination before the architect ever got to work on it. He had planned every corner guided by the experience of his present house and his concept of the ideal one. He had saved money, had made his calculations time and time again, trimming budgets and straining resources; had spoken about it day after day, with his wife first and then with friends and acquaintances who had recently built their own houses and could offer views and experience and, above all, the priceless opportunity to talk the matter over and fix his own ideas while listening to theirs. And when finally the figures tallied, the plans emerged, the dream became a concrete possibility, and the decision was taken, he went to work on it with all his heart, toiled through every sketch, sweat through every brick—and saw at long last the dream of his life come true in iron and concrete and wood and glass, and moved to the new house as though he were moving into heaven for a lifetime of bliss. Earthly rehearsal of eternal joy.

A friend of mine once went through that experience, and I had the chance to follow it close to him, right up to the snag that developed at the end and endangered for a time the whole project so carefully prepared. It became quite a delicate problem. He had been living all his life in the old quarter of an ancient city built by the Arabs inside protective walls, a labyrinth of narrow lanes and small dark houses crowded together in physical defense against the rays of the sun and the raids of the enemy. Now he had completed the building of a new house in the airy outskirts of the growing township, and was ready to move into it on the auspicious date carefully fixed by an astrologer in consultation with the stars. But then the problem came up: His old widowed mother refused to move into the new premises. She was shown the new place with all its conveniences, running water and clean air, privacy and comfort, a balcony and a garden, and even a temple just in front of the house in which to worship daily, an unusual and happy advantage that—her son had thought—would easily persuade his devout mother to accept the change. Yet she refused. And her words were clear and definite: "I want to die in my house." *My house.* The familiarity of old corners and used drawers. And, deeper than that, the symbol of old ideas and cherished principles. "My house" stands for my values, my tastes, my life. For the old woman to leave her house meant to leave the protection of her habits and beliefs, her atmosphere and her mentality. She could not be expected to do that in old age—to change her surroundings of mind and body, and go to live in another's house; to see things from another person's point of view, even if that person was her own son. And so she refused. And meanwhile, pulling in the opposite direction but for the very same reason—that is, to find his own expression, his own personality and his own freedom—the son was eager to move into the house he had designed and built for himself. He was eager to begin his new and independent life, of which his new house was symbol and expression. But he could not leave his mother alone in the old house, and so postponed indefinitely the shifting to the new one. He said resignedly, "I'll have to wait till my mother dies to go to live in my own house." And when I heard him say those words they sounded in my ears as though he had said, "I'll have to wait till my mother dies to begin to live my own life." Such was indeed the case with him.

One day I received the visit of a middle-aged woman I had

never met before, and whose purpose in coming to see me she did not immediately reveal to me. On her visiting card was a very common name that told me nothing about her. She came and spoke to me for a long time about many things, as though exploring approaches and testing the ground. I could not see what she was driving at, but she was cultured and refined, and I kept up the pleasant exchange with a vague expectation of something I could not clearly define. After a good long time at conversation, she kept silent for a little while, threw her head back, laughed openly and said, "I think I'm going to trust you. I'm going to tell you something nobody around here knows about me. I am a granddaughter of . . . ," and she pronounced one of the greatest names in recent world history. My eyes registered surprise; she acknowleged it and continued: "For years I lived under the burden of that name. My introduction to anybody brought at once the respectful nod, the knowing smile, the awed silence. I liked it at the beginning. It was good to be noticed. But soon I hated it. I was only somebody's granddaughter. I was expected to think, speak, act like my grandfather. I was constantly reminded that I had to live up to the name I bore. In other words, I was told I had to be somebody else. I was not me. I did respect my grandfather, but I was not going to surrender my personality to him. I went to live in another part of the country, married outside our circle, adopted my husband's surname and settled in a place where nobody knew me. There I developed as I wanted to develop, and today, after many years, I have felt free to tell someone about my family ties. Now you know."

Yes, I knew and I appreciated. The burden of a great name can be oppressive. And, in a less dramatic but no less effective way, the burden of *any* name, of family and heritage, of tradition and custom, of parents and society can be as oppressive and damaging to a person's development and growth. The burden of the past, the need to conform, the pressure to obey. The danger is all the greater because the values and usages one is required to conform to are often true and beneficent in themselves, and so the doubt arises whether one accepts them because of their own worth or because of outside pressure. No wonder that in the struggle to find one's own identity, crises come and excesses are committed as though to test the genuineness of one's own convictions. Growing pains in man's endless search.

One extreme case, known to history though often silenced in well-meaning biographies, is that of Mahatma Gandhi's own young son. To defy his father and manifest his rebellion against him he took to a licentious life and went to the radical extent of publicly changing his religion—an unthinkable step to his pious father. He wanted to dissociate himself from his saintly father who, according to him, had tried to impose his sanctity on him. When he misbehaved, his father fasted for him in open atonement; and, to the son, this was a way of bringing pressure to bear upon him so that the unseemly behavior of a dissolute son would not tarnish the official image of the father of the nation. Without judging father or son, I see in them a telling example of the tension created when one generation, with the best of intentions, tries to impose its values on the next. The search for identity and the need for independence may override every other instinct and bring suffering to the best of families. Gandhi's son died a pitiful death in a public hospital.

This is a problem not only for teenagers, not only just within the family, and not only when there is a sharp and open clash. It actually becomes more dangerous when it goes underground, when the tension becomes subconscious and grows darkly throughout the years, gathering momentum as the person matures and seeks his or her own personality within and against family, society, profession, and/or religion. Though in truth it is not necessarily a problem; it is a gift, a privilege, a dawn. It is the awakening of the soul in personal wonder to the innermost reality of its own worth. This urge to be oneself, when it surfaces with all its might and challenge in a person's life, is the precious and dangerous opportunity to break through to a new birth and make life the unique, personal, individual adventure it is meant to be for each man and woman in this lovely world.

3

The View from the Window

We conform to common usage because we find it convenient and safe, and, once we have conformed, we like those who come after us to conform to it too, so that we can continue to feel comfortable and safe in their company. Follow the current, do as all do and think what all think. Be one with the crowd, and you will see what the crowd sees and reach where the crowd reaches—which will be good enough for most people in easy acquiescence, but will leave unsatisfied the eyes that can see more and the feet that are eager to walk farther.

In almost any city of the world today one can see groups of tourists who see the sights together under the practical arrangement of a fixed itinerary, a daily program, and a common fee. They all follow a guide who explains to them in their own language—ready translation of memorized landmarks—the history of what they see and the meaning of what they hear. They all look right when they are told to look right, and left when their guide points left, in a rhythmical unison of murmured approval. Sometimes, when they walk away from the safety of their bus, the guide raises a small flag for all to see and to follow around the corners of a street or through the galleries of a museum. The group stays together and nobody is lost. Day by day they follow their schedule, and, as their expression goes, they "do" a city, a country, sometimes a whole continent in record time with professional thoroughness. They all go back safely home with a stack of pictures, souvenirs, and videotapes to prove their presence on the chosen spots and boast of their trip to their friends.

Convenient, no doubt. Prepaid, programmed, guaranteed. But, for the same reason, uninspiring and commonplace. The picture postcards are the same for every tourist, the souvenirs cheap and repetitious. However marvelous the country may be, there is hardly any knowledge of a new land, any contact with new people when one has traveled in the insured isolation of a conducted tour.

Most people's journey through life is a conducted tour. They look where they are told to look and they see what they are told to see. They go where they are taken and they stay there while they are kept there. Willful obedience to a prearranged routine. Look to your right. Look to your left. A unison of heads in an ocean of ideas. Study what you are told to study, learn what you are told to learn; value what you are told to value, pursue what you are told to pursue; make money, seek pleasure, achieve fame, look smart; clap when all clap and smile when all smile; don't ask questions and don't rock the boat. Follow your guide and you will be safe. Your guardian, your party, your teacher, your guru: Look at his little flag and you will not be lost. Never mind if you miss the thrill of discovery and the personal experience of the wonder of life. You will be safely back at the appointed place on the appointed day.

Fortunately the door is still open and the way is cleared for those who want to explore life on their own, to travel unusual paths and let themselves be surprised by the turns of the mind, the skylines of the spirit, and the landscapes of the soul. They are ready to travel alone, to risk danger and brave hardships; they love adventure and trust their hearts in the bewildering maze that life on earth is. They are perpetual pioneers who, while respecting the group and recognizing the advantages of a common trip, choose for themselves the legitimate privilege of a personal search. They like to experience the feel of new soil under bare feet, they love to breathe new air and taste new food, they welcome the gentle panic of getting lost for a while in an alien land. Tourism on a shoestring budget. Hitchhiking on the roads that lead to heaven. The days of the great explorers are not over yet.

A person who has not discovered new land for himself will not easily acquiesce in the discovery of new lands by others. He may see in their discoveries a rebuke to his mental laziness and a challenge to his own inertia. And so he is likely to oppose their ways and attack their conclusions, to justify his lack of achievements by nullifying those of others. I did not do it, therefore it was not worth doing, and if someone else does it I will put him down so that I may not be exposed and my reputation not suffer. People who themselves do not change are not likely to allow others to change, or to tolerate change in others. Thus they oppose change, society grows formal, and ideas harden. It takes courage, in that atmosphere, to risk originality and express dissidence. Most people will always prefer silence to confrontation.

A great man of letters is said to have declared on his deathbed that Homer bored him. It was almost a last-hour confession to get rid of the guilty feeling that had been brought on him by a secret disagreement with the judgment of mankind at large. Literary mankind held that Homer was its greatest epic poet, and so his literary virtues had to be extolled, and, what is worse, his poems had to be enjoyed. But the dying man had never succeeded in doing that. He had repeatedly tried to read the Iliad and the Odyssey, and they had fallen from his hands. He had kept his disappointment to himself. How could he declare that Homer bored him when all cultured people around him clearly enjoyed his works (or so they said) and proclaimed them to be the best epics ever written by the hand of man? There would definitely have been a perception of something wrong with him if he had differed from the universal opinion of men and women of letters everywhere. Something would appear to be lacking in him if he was not able to appreciate Homer as others did, and so he dissembled, nodded his head, and at most kept discreetly quiet when others sang the old bard's praises. He saw nothing where others saw marvels. Could his eyes be at fault? No. His eyes were not sick, and his literary taste was not wanting; only, it was different. And it takes courage to be different in a society that prizes conformity and rewards compliance. So he had kept his opinion to himself, labored through life under the burden of his concealed rebellion, and finally cleared his soul at the last moment with the public announcement: Homer bores me. Then he died in peace.

Sometimes our hearts too would feel unburdened and our souls would find peace if only we could express in candid sincerity our humble disagreement with mankind at large. If we could say "I respect the judgments of centuries and honor the opinions of wise men around me; I know the verdicts of critics and the tastes of knowledgeable people; but I know also my own inner tastes and my personal convictions, and I make bold to declare, without arrogance and without offense, that Homer bores me. I see no point in forcing myself to see what I do not see and to feel what I do not feel. On the contrary, I believe I can contribute more to the richness of thought and the variety of life around me by my honest dissent than by my forced acquiescence. Here is my opinion and my experience, for what they are worth. Let those who so desire take notice of them, and let the others ignore them. And let old Homer by all means keep his throne undisturbed." (I, for one, enjoy his works immensely.)

In practice, however, this attitude is not so easy to take, and we may find it more expedient to say with everybody that Homer is wonderful and his epics most enjoyable—which to many people they undoubtedly are but not to all. We repeat what all have repeated before us, and old views are strengthened with new acceptance. Mankind may be the poorer for that.

Here is a modern parable to stir up ripples of unease in alert minds. In a jail where convicts lived in strict seclusion only one room had a window through which a person could see a beautiful landscape of mountains and trees and clouds, and watch sunrises and sunsets in their ever-changing glory. From the rest of the prison, with its high walls and narrow cells, no such view was possible. By tradition that privileged room was occupied by the seniormost convict, and when he was released, the next in seniority came to live in it. Also by tradition the man who occupied that room told the others about the wonderful view he watched from his bed, and described sunrises and sunsets for those who could enjoy them only through his words. Those descriptions of the landscape, in its different moods and seasons, by the seniormost convict—conscious of his responsibility and careful to use his best art—were the highlight of the limited entertainment provided by the prison. The room was coveted, and the waiting list carefully followed.

One day the room was vacated, and the next convict in line got ready to move into it. It had been a long wait, and he was eager to see for himself the view he had so often heard described, and to tell it now to others in his turn, enriching the experience with his own style, his own perception of beauty and his own power of description. He had been starved of beauty and nature, and was eager to make up for it for himself and the others with the view from the window. It had been a long wait, and now at last it was about to bear fruit. He shifted his belongings to the privileged room, was left alone in it, and finally approached the window with reverent expectation. He looked out of the window, and all he saw in front of him was a high wall at arm's length that obliterated every view whichever way he turned his eyes. The sad truth dawned on him with irresistible finality. There was no view from the window. There were no trees and no mountains, no sunrises and no sunsets. There was only a flat, coarse, wall, and that was all that had ever been there. He had been cheated, and with him all the inmates of the prison from time immemorial. The disappointment was final.

He felt anger and frustration, and waited impatiently for the moment he would come out of the room, meet his jail companions, and tell them the truth. If he had been the victim of a tactless joke, he would at least be the first to expose the farce that had been going on for generations among those unfortunate people. He would put an end to the legend, bury the fiction, make all forget forever the false glories of the room with a window. Thus there would be no more anxiety to get to it, no more quarrels, no jealousy and no hurry. There was nothing special in the room, and there was no point in waiting anxiously for it.

He came out of the room and met the eager crowd. They were all looking at him with the expectation of a new experience, of a new narrative from the lips of a man who had seen the sight for the first time and must be full of it and anxious to share it with those who could enjoy it only through his words. He looked into their faces, paused awhile and then said: "There are no words to describe what I saw from the window. In front of me was a line of trees, heavy with green leaves that murmured softly in the wings of the wind; behind them stretched a garden of flowers of every kind and color as far as my eyes could reach; and then on the far horizon a range of snow-capped mountains that seemed to reach up to heaven. It is the most wonderful sight I have ever seen. It was worth waiting for, for so long. I'll keep telling you faithfully the changes I observe in the marvelous landscape, and will describe for you the sunrises and sunsets as they visit me in all their glory day by day through that truly blessed window."

The other convicts nodded their grateful appreciation, and the legend went on.

4

Body and Mind

I mentioned in the first chapter that a seventeen-year-old, and otherwise healthy, young man could not walk because he had not been taught how to do so. It seems at first an unlikely proposition, and yet it is plainly evident: Man has to learn even how to walk, and without a long and painstaking training he cannot perform what seems to be the simplest of his actions, which is to walk on his legs. Nerves have to be directed, muscles have to be coordinated, limbs have to be coaxed, and very slowly and very awkwardly, after many false starts and many falls, the human child finally begins to walk . . . and soon forgets how hard it was for him to learn that elementary task.

Everything I do now is something I have learned through a long process. Even what seems to me spontaneous is a carefully acquired reflex. Nothing is more natural for me than to extend my arm and catch a ball that is thrown at me. I do not realize anymore that it took me years to master that simple move. Once I was playing ball with a six-year-old girl. She was big enough, and eager to enjoy the game she herself had proposed. I first threw the ball at an angle to make the game more interesting, but I saw at once that I had overestimated her prowess. I began then to throw the ball slowly and directly right in front of her. Even so she had difficulty in catching it. She had not yet progressed in the elementary art. I watched her carefully as she strained her eyes, moved her arm stiffly without action at the elbow or at the wrist, missed the ball and laughed merrily at her own awkwardness. The training of the eye to measure the distance, the movement of the arm to meet the ball, the exact angle, the split-second timing are all infinitely complicated skills that have taken our systems a long time to learn in childhood. We forget the process, take the result for granted and call it "natural." Nothing is natural. The simplest physical movement is comparable in nature if not in degree to a Ph.D. thesis: It has taken time, effort, and concentration to be programmed into our inner circuits.

When a grown-up suffers a stroke he or she loses the faculty of movement in part of the body. If physical damage has not occurred the use of the limbs can be recovered, but only through a long and repetitious retraining which will be both humiliating and painful. The muscles and nerves are there as they were the day before the stroke, but the circuit in the brain that was responsible for those movements is gone, and to replace it is a laborious process. To see an adult person going through an elementary reeducation to regain the use of his or her arms and legs is a chastening experience and an important lesson. Nothing in us is spontaneous. Everything we have or do is learned and acquired.

This conditioning of my muscles for posture and movement is beneficent and essential. I could hardly live a human life without it. What is important is to realize the price we pay for it. Every conditioning is a limitation, a curtailment, a censorship. You are enabled to do this . . . at the expense of giving up other possibilities and other ways. Muscles are close to nerves, and nerves carry sensations; therefore the conditioning of my muscles affects my emotions, and through them my character. There is no such a thing as an innocent conditioning. Each service carries its price tag. As a Westerner I have been trained to walk fast, and that has imprinted a brisk step upon my whole life, my thought, my work, my hurry to get things done and to reach places, to obtain results with quick efficiency and purposeful resolve. On the other hand, an Indian has been taught to squat since childhood, and in that primeval posture, close to the earth from which he comes and recollected in the linking of his body, he learns patience and peace, lives in cosmic contemplation, and waits for eternity. The shaping of our muscles has resulted in the shaping of our minds. A whole way of life has already been inscribed into my bones and sinews by the very way I have been taught to walk, to stand, to sit. And if such a harmless exercise has already marked my life and steered my thoughts, I begin to think with curious anticipation of the more direct and concerted ways in which society and tradition have bent into submission not only my hands and feet but my values and tastes. A long conspiracy to be unraveled thread by thread.

Thérèse Bertherat in her book *The Body Has Its Reasons* presents a striking example that has made me think. An old woman had lived the last years of her life with her body bent at right angles at the waist, so that she could walk only while leaning on a stick, with her face looking downward. Her bones and joints had hardened into that position, and she could never unbend. When she died, people mused that a special coffin in the shape of a right angle would be needed, as her body would not fit into a straight structure. Such a coffin, however, was not needed. Immediately after her death, before rigor mortis had set in, it was found that her dead body unbent smoothly and naturally and became straight again, almost by itself. There was nothing wrong with the bones and joints. The bones had not set. It was the muscles, in the enslaving tension of a tormented existence, that had held fast the bones in an unnatural bend. When death deprived the muscles of their grip, the bones became free again and the body straightened out without difficulty.

To me this is an almost fearful thought. I think of the muscles of my body, stiff and hardened through years of discipline, rigidity and rigor, wooden postures and straight carriage. I was trained to walk erect, be proud of a ramrod stance, shackle my hands into polite restraint, keep my eyes on the floor a short distance ahead of my feet. A prize was given for being able to sit for hours without a stir, to kneel in prayer like a stone statue, to control each movement with what was called "religious maturity." Indeed! I can feel my muscles all curled up around nerves and bones, unyielding taskmasters within my own body. A message of intolerance has been written into my own tissues through the severe conditioning of regimented upbringing. The whole network of inner communication between head and members, brain and movement, has been taken over by a foreign army in forced occupation. And the crux of the problem and the pathos of the situation is that I have not realized it, and still believe that the network is in my hands. Unless I wake up to the fact that I do not rule myself, I shall not stir and mobilize my resources to regain control in my own life. I have to sense my own dependence, if ever I have to win independence.

Buckminster Fuller, genial inventor of the geodesic dome with all its architectural beauty and geometric perfection, tells how one day his own young daughter drew his attention to the rigidity of his body and the stiffness of his movements. He had never thought of it before, having considered his bodily behavior thoroughly becoming; but now the pointed criticism of a person who knew and loved him well was a revelation to him; he believed that it had a great influence in releasing suppleness in his body and, through it, into his unique architectural creations. This is how he described his experience. "When my daughter, Allegra, was twelve years old, she told me: 'Daddy, you were brought up as a Bostonian gentleman for whom any motion of the body is considered ill-mannered. As a United States Naval Officer, you were taught to carry yourself stiffly erect, and that any motion must have official meaning.' Allegra went on to say, 'My body wants to talk all the time. I like your ideas, Daddy, I like your philosophy. I think you are greatly frustrating the effectiveness of your thinking by your self-suppression.' I was so impressed with what she said that I set about at the age of thirty-nine to unlock myself. It made a very great difference in my life, as my post-1940 history will show."

"My body wants to talk all the time." These are beautiful words. Each body wants to talk, it has its own language, it can show joy and grief, it can achieve instant communication and reach deeply into emotion and meaning. There is a grammar of gesture and touch, of look and smile, that transcends all words and enhances all messages with the genuine sense of a total expression. Unfortunately our bodies have been shackled by custom and formality, and they express only the "official meanings" that ultimately are no meanings at all. Our handshakes are mechanical, and our smiles are programmed. A frozen body is the result of a misguided training, and now in turn is the permanent source of unnatural behavior in our daily encounters with other men and women as programmed as we are to look without seeing and touch without feeling. Most of us act and move most of the time like well-behaved robots, and the common patterns in society around us make us forget the long conditioning that has resulted in the stereotyped behavior that dampens our reactions and impoverishes our lives. To realize the extent of our bondage is the first step toward liberation from it.

A simple consideration can go a long way toward understanding the way our physiology is conditioned by early training, and the influence such a conditioning exerts on our lives. Few people master the pronunciation of a foreign language unless they learned it in childhood. Our throat, our vocal cords, our tongue, our lips, and our whole mouth are all shaped in such a way by the learning of our mother tongue that for the rest of our lives we can emit with ease only the sounds of our homeland while we find it almost impossible to reproduce the strange utterances of people from other regions. Our vocal cords are initially virgin and flexible, but, once they are set to one tune, they just refuse to play another. In the Gujarati language in India there are four *t*'s, not to mention the several combinations among them; yet a staunch co-worker of mine, of Spanish origin, sturdily asserts that for him there is only one *t*, and he leaves it to his listeners to sort out which one is to be understood in each case. A professor and author of a dictionary on pronunciation once asked a Spanish student in his class his name, and when the student said proudly, "Ridruejo," the professor almost went into a trance and requested of him: "Please, say that again. What a phonetic treat for British ears!" The initial heavily trilled *r*, and the guttural *j* of Arab origin, are sounds seldom to be heard on the British Isles. And in Rome, before the second Vatican Council, there was a bit of a stir when a rumor spread that an American bishop was saying Mass in English, which was strictly forbidden at the time. It turned out, however, that the good bishop was actually using Latin in his liturgy, but that his Latin, pronounced with a heavy Southern drawl, sounded to musical Italian ears like a barbarian language they took to be English. Unavoidable confusion in a Babel of tongues.

Now, this is a matter for thought. Everybody knows the close connection that exists between language and mentality. The whole culture is reflected in the language, and the language in turn shapes new minds into their ancestral culture. The fact, then, that my throat finds it difficult to pronounce other sounds, is both a symbol and a conditioning factor of rigidity in my thoughts and views as it is in my vowels and consonants. My throat refuses to utter new sounds, as my mind refuses to accept new points of view. I cannot accept as mine what I cannot pronounce with ease. My vocal cords, while rendering me the distinct service of allowing me to talk, have subtly and effectively limited my world of expression—and with it my world of perception and understanding, my capacity to feel at home with other people and in other cultures. I am a slave to my pronunciation.

An organic conditioning marks me for life. The way those tiny muscles have been tuned determines the music I am going to sing and to enjoy while I am in this body. Again, the music is fine, but I want a larger repertory. In the matter of music and of language, there is no question of forgetting one's mother tongue; there is the question of learning new ones: the languages of the mind.

My whole organism has been conditioned to do, enjoy, accept, prize, repeat certain things and to reject others. This is not a conscious process anymore, but a preprogrammed choice that is triggered by the cells within me before I know what is happening in the recesses of my mind. It is the automatic pilot that steers its course without any reference to me, though I am in the cockpit. The method is comfortable and safe, but good only for a routine flight. Now I want to explore new horizons and charter new routes. While thanking my muscles and nerves and neurons and dendrites for their unfailing service in the past, I want to let them know that from now on I will call the shots and sit at the helm. I want to reown my organism and bring to the movements of my body and my soul a new spontaneity and a new grace. I want to unwind before it is too late. I do not want people to have to worry about the shape of my coffin.

5

On Roses and Fish

Once I was giving a talk to a group of Indians in New York, and during the talk a collection was taken for the association that had organized the function. While I kept talking, a small girl, barely three or four years old, carrying a basket almost bigger than herself, walked in between the rows of chairs and collected the contributions of the listeners. I was looking at her while I talked, and I observed a peculiarity in her behavior. When people put single dollar bills into the basket, she left them undisturbed; but when a ten-dollar or even a higher denomination bill landed in her basket she promptly took it and put it in her own pocket. Smart girl, I thought. Unfortunately for her, her mother was also watching her, noticed the maneuver, and moved quickly to undo the girl's moves. She took all the bills from her pocket, restored them to the basket, and saw to it that the basket with all its contents was duly delivered to the treasurer of the association. The talk proceeded without further incidents, but the lesson of that evening remained in my memory. That little girl knew the value of money, knew the difference between a one-dollar and a ten-dollar bill, and knew that a ten-dollar bill was something worth keeping in one's pocket. An early lesson in practical economics.

The girl's mother acted fast to correct her daughter's mischief. But then, the person responsible for the mischief was the mother. Where else but at home had the small girl learned the importance of money? Later in life people will say about her, as we all say about everybody else, that she is money-minded, and maybe her own parents will complain about that. But it is from them that she took the cue. Money was a value in her home, the word was often spoken, the care shown, the dollar bills treated with reverence as family gods. And she learned the worship. Home is the first source of values for the human child.

Even if that girl rebels against her parents when she grows up, despises her cult of money and becomes a hippie, she will be only reacting to the training she has been given, and her reaction is as much a conditioning as her acceptance. Reaction is only acceptance with its sign changed. Whether in submission or in rebellion she is following (in one direction or another) a marked path. She does not have the free horizon of multiple choice, but the predetermined groove of a single track. And money is only an example. In morals and in etiquette, in religion and in politics she has received a similar training at home—the first training in life that works on a virgin mind and therefore imprints itself on it with privileged priority.

The influence of the home in the formation of the person is obvious and universally recognized. The Gestalt school of psychology uses the word "introjection," Transactional Analysis speaks of "parental injunctions" and Rational Emotive Therapy of "tapes," but the reality is the same. The important point is to realize the non-conscious, non-critical character of the transference of values. The child takes it all in, and believes that this is *the* way it is done, and that all other ways are inferior and the people who follow them are second-rate people. There is no questioning, no evaluation, no hesitation. This is the true path, because this is the one we follow at home, and my parents know. Fritz Perls graphically describes "introjection" as "swallowing without chewing." I have swallowed the morsel whole, and now it has entered me, but I have not chewed it, I have not assimilated it, I have not converted it into my own flesh and blood. It is in me but not part of me; it is a foreign body within my life boundaries. That belief, that practice, that preference, that judgment—each pops up when its particular stimulus comes, but I am hardly responsible for them. The tape has been played, that is all. And the tape had been put there by someone else. It is time to revise the tapes in my mind and keep only those I really mean to keep, those that have truly become mine through subsequent experience and conviction. I do not want to live on borrowed material.

Once I witnessed a heated argument between two Indian housewives on whether or not solidified sugar-cane juice should be added to the sauce that goes with the rice. Each spoke with a vehemence and conviction that made the exchange seem a matter of life and death. For one of them the juice definitely had to be used, and without it there was no proper meal, whereas for the other the very thought of it was anathema. The explanation, of course, was very simple. One of the ladies came from Gujarat, where the juice is added, while the other came from the Punjab where it is not. The Gujarati housewife had seen sugar-cane juice mixed into the brew all her life, and could not imagine or conceive of it being done in any other way. If she would neglect that rubric in her cooking, she would be sharply reproved by all at home. The Punjabi housewife, on the contrary, had never seen or tasted such a thing, and for her it would be a culinary blunder to attempt such a mixture. Both were right. Both were defending their own kitchen traditions. And both were proclaiming in the vehemence of their arguments that they had seldom eaten outside their own homes. The matter of sugar-cane juice is, of course, of minor importance, in spite of the energy the two housewives spent on it; but the situation can become serious and thought-provoking when we discuss principles and behavior. It is always important to keep in mind where we come from. We can save ourselves a good many quarrels.

It is not only the concrete ideas or facts that shape our minds, but the air we breathe and the atmosphere we live in. I heard the following story from Ravishankar Maharaj, the popular saint who lived to be one hundred and two with the sanity of his social sense and the wit of his stories. Three fisherwomen went daily from the fishing village to the market town to sell fish. One day, on their way back, they were caught in a storm and took refuge in a house by the wayside. The owner of the house was a kind man and invited them to spend the night in his house, as the storm kept raging. He laid three cots for them in a room, and left them to their sleep. After a while, however, he noticed that the women were restless, and went to inquire what the matter was. He found them awake and agitated, and they told him in answer to his questions: "We cannot sleep. We are sorry, but there is a heavy stench in this room and that has taken away our sleep. We cannot bear the smell." The man was surprised and hurt. "Bad smell? In my house? Everything is clean here, and I have even brought these roses into the room for you. I am a gardener, and take pride in my flowers." The women nodded: "Yes, that is it. Those flowers you say, those roses. They smell. We cannot bear such a foul smell. We cannot sleep in this room."

When Ravishankar Maharaj told that story he smiled mischievously at the end, and drew no conclusions. He knew he had told a dangerous story. The smell of raw fish and the smell of fresh roses. Which is the good one and which is the bad one? It all depends on your nose. And the nose goes by the smells familiar to it in childhood and classified from the start as "good" or "bad." For the gardener the scent of his roses is pride and delight; for the fisherwoman the pungent odor of the fish her husband catches is livelihood and bounty. Perfume or stench is only a label fixed by the mind on a neutral smell. The trouble is that we, on the gardener's side, consider the smell of roses as obviously, objectively, essentially good in itself for all people and forever; while we classify with the same ease and definiteness the smell of raw fish as repulsive in itself by virtue of its own composition and the very nature of things. This is not so. The labels are arbitrary. We may choose, of course, the smells we like and we may avoid as far as we can those that are now offensive to us; but we'll do well to remember all the while that there is nothing inborn, instinctive, universal about good and bad smells.

Ravishankar Maharaj ended his story by saying slowly, knowingly, lovingly: "Good smell? Bad smell? Who can tell?"

6

Extreme Conditioning

We all readily see that we are subject to a certain amount of conditioning and that it is desirable to get rid of it as far as possible. What we do not see so easily is the extent and the depth of this conditioning, and the alarming proportions it has grown to in our lives. And unless we realize the extent of the damage we are not likely to rise up and try our best to undo it.

One way to realize the lengths to which conditioning can go is to analyze it in extreme cases. And one such case, unfortunately common in our times, is the case of the terrorist. His action in killing innocent people in cold blood is condemned as cruel, wicked, inhuman, and criminal by the whole of society. What is more, to all upright people it is incomprehensible and absurd. How can he do that? How can he murder men, women and children, who have nothing to do in the matter, just to draw attention to his cause and bring pressure to bear upon it, whatever it may be? Modern society has still to grapple with the problem of terrorism, and the first step is to understand the mentality of the person who kills. As a humorist has said with dry irony: We have explained the transition from ape to man; now we have to explain the transition from man to terrorist. The key concept for that understanding is the terrorist's conditioning. To go a little deeper into the matter may help us to understand this unfortunate person who has become a phenomenon of our times, and to understand also another unfortunate reality of our own lives: the terrorist we all carry within us. The increasing violence in a civilized world.

An active member of a terrorist band was caught by the police one day and his story came out. It was a revealing story. He was a young man, fully committed to his group's cause including its violent expression in terrorist activities. He had helped prepare several such actions, but had not yet taken part in any direct killing with his own hands. It was then discovered that he had cancer, and the doctors informed him he had only a short time to live. He then approached the head of his band and asked to be entrusted with a direct action at least once before his death. He did not want to die unfulfilled, he said, to die without having killed first in the promotion of his holy cause. One killing, at least, would justify his life and he could then die at peace. Unfortunately for him he was caught when he was preparing his kamikaze action, and died of cancer before he could kill with a bomb.

While reading that piece of news I felt a shock wave go through me. I understand that a person might like to do a signal good work before he or she dies—to go on a pilgrimage to a holy place, to establish a foundation for service or enlightenment, to settle satisfactorily his or her children in marriage, to build a church or a library. A person may want to do something that will be good for others and that will make people remember him or her and be grateful to that memory for some time to come. That may even be viewed as the fulfillment of the person's life, and satisfaction may be experienced when this aim is achieved. But this was something different. This was another wish, another man. He wants to kill before he dies, and he calls that the fulfillment of his life. A trail of blood. A legacy of murder. The broken bodies of innocent victims, and the wails without relief of the loved ones they have left behind. A crime without name. A mean deed. An irredeemable madness. And yet, for him, that absurd action is what would give meaning to his whole life.

What for others was unthinkable, was obvious for him; what others rejected as an unmitigated evil, he embraced as a noble deed. How to explain that topsy-turvy world in which such a person lives?

That terrorist has been told from childhood that his people suffer an unjust oppression, that they are a minority against the mighty powers that enslave them, that they have the right and the duty to fight for justice and freedom, that the only way left to them is the way of violence—and that therefore those who, with danger to themselves, take up violence for this just cause, are servants of the people and martyrs to the cause. This is the atmosphere in which the future terrorist is brought up, the words he hears daily, the ideals that are hammered into him. This is the conditioning, or—to use a word I have been avoiding so far, but that finds its rightful place here—the brainwashing. This is the way he is taught to think, to act, to respond instinctively when the issues come up. Hijacking and kidnapping become his commandments, and bombs and machine guns the tools of his trade. The risk of placing the bomb is a heroic act, and the massacre of women and children a just sacrifice. He sees it that way, he thinks that way, he is convinced that it is the right way, and he is ready to give his life for it. To himself and his people he is a martyr. Strange martyr who kills instead of being killed, but that is the way they see it. The kidnappers of the Kuwait Airlines plane in 1988 called the long agony of the imprisoned passengers "the flight of martyrdom." These terrorists were suffering and thus making others suffer for their cause. It was that conviction that gave them the strength and courage to go through with their plan amidst dangers and fatigue. They were martyrs on a holy mission, or so they appeared to themselves.

Another terrorist was once on his way to plant a bomb in a public place where its blast would have killed a number of innocent people. The bomb, however, exploded in his hands before he reached the place, and he alone was killed by it. A Mass was offered for him at his home parish with the attendance of many people, and the parish priest in his homily compared the terrorist—who had died "in an act of service"—to Jesus who gave his life for his brothers. After the Mass, a public procession was taken to proclaim and honor the dead terrorist as a martyr. Again, that news item provoked the indignation of sane people for whom equating the terrorist with Jesus was sheer blasphemy. But it was not so for the people of that parish. Extreme conditioning, but real and actual. They had been differently conditioned because they lived in a different world, and thus they judged things differently. Each one is a child of one's own conditioning.

In a way Jesus had prepared us for this. He told his disciples: "A day will come when people will kill you thinking they are doing a service to God." This is exactly what is happening. People kill in the name of God, in the name of the group, in the name of the cause. In other words, they kill with a good conscience. The one obvious rule of social behavior which is respect for the lives of others becomes obliterated by the cloud that covers the view of fanatic men. They honestly believe they are doing a service to God when they kill people who, in their court without appeal, they have decided should die. Strange but true. And they do that because their mentality, their upbringing, their conditioning lead them to believe that that is the right thing to do. We profoundly deplore their stand. But we cannot deny their honesty in some cases.

Times without number I have heard it said when the theme of terrorism comes up or when the news of another attack stirs again the indignation of people of peace: How can they do that? How can they shoot a man through his back in cold blood? How can they plant a bomb in a crowded shop? How can they keep a man in bondage for months or years on end? How can they be so wicked, so senseless, so inhuman? How can there be so much

malice, so much hatred, so much evil in a man's heart? We just
cannot understand how a human being in his senses can act in
this way.

My answer, proposed with tentative humility and sincere soul-
searching, is that, regrettable though the terrorist's action undoubtedly is, it is not beyond understanding. In fact, in that
understanding lies the only possible solution of the problem, if it
ever is to be found in this troubled world. The terrorist is, in his
way, logical, consistent, even reasonable, however hard it is for
us to say so. He is only drawing a conclusion from the premises
that have been imprinted in his mind; he is only acting according to the conditioning he has received. True, the conditioning
should not be there (which is precisely my whole point), but
once it is, it works itself out with blind inevitability. Nothing is
gained by our refusing to understand the situation and saying
that it is absurd. It is painful, yes, but not precisely absurd. A
way to a solution could be opened if we were to say instead: We
understand the circumstances and prejudices that have led this
man to indulge in violence, and, while condemning his action,
we realize its background and we endeavor to look for the possible solution. The solution is to tackle the conditioning so as to
suppress its effects. How this can be done is another matter, but
my point is that merely expressing condemnation and declaring
that we do not understand how men can act this way is of no
help. On the contrary, we may conceivably help if we realize the
role that conditioning plays in a person's life. The terrorist need
not be wicked, may be only committed to a cause. He may not be
torturing men gratuitously, but may be working painfully for an
ideal. We regret with all our heart the human suffering he causes,
but we note his position and understand his motivation, however unfortunate. True, human motives and selfish gains will be
intermingled in the terrorist's case, but so they are also in anybody else's case. The answer to violence is not in proclaiming it
senseless, but in understanding its background.

This is, of course, no defense of terrorism, but only an attempt to realize the havoc caused by conditioning when carried out to its baleful extreme. Once a person is placed in the mental climate and cultural surroundings that favor a certain course of action, he or she will eventually take it, however painful or absurd it may be in itself. For that person it has ceased to be absurd, because it is seen from a different standpoint.

Violence is the ultimate mistake man can make on earth. Yet even violence can become a consciously pursued goal when a corresponding conditioning has prepared the mind to accept it. This extreme example reveals to us the power that conditioning exerts on the human mind, and may motivate us to better understand its workings so as to guard ourselves from its dangers.

7

The Secret of Fashion

Another type of conditioning, less sharp but more universal, is fashion. This represents the need to conform, to dress in a particular way not because I like it, but because everybody else dresses that way; to wear my hair in a particular style not because that particular style appeals to me but because it is the style of those I live with and want to be accepted by. Though, of course, very soon I start telling everybody, and myself in the first place, that I like it and it is the most wonderful style ever invented, so different from those old-fashioned things other people wear, and from the things we ourselves wore only last year. And so we have the curious phenomenon of a group of people who all wear clothes none of them likes, in an effort each of them makes to be accepted by everybody else. In a witty cartoon two girls stand before a shop's window in which next season's fashions are exhibited, and they tell each other with mournful countenance: "See what awful things we'll have to wear this year!" The cartoon does not show the next step: They go into the shop and buy the clothing.

Fashion works because people, particularly young people, have an overwhelming need to belong to their group, to be accepted by their peers, to feel they are not alone in the world but are supported by people like themselves. Now, to belong to that group they have to conform to the way people in that group speak, act, and dress. That is the expected behavior of a member of the group. Follow it, and you are in. You may like it or not, but that is the price you have to pay to enter the compulsory fraternity. Wear yellow if all wear yellow (if you dislike the color, you'll come to like it), and grow long hair because they wear it long. Fashion is a passport to acceptance, a seal that proclaims to the world, and chiefly to the person in need of support: You are one of us, because you dress like us and talk like us and drink like us. Conformity to fashion gives security (however flimsy and artificial this security may in fact be), and the young person desperately needs a sense of security in this lonely world. To wear jeans where all wear jeans, and broad belts where all wear broad belts; how well can the young man or woman now mix with the crowd, be one with the group, disappear in the safe anonymity of dozens of people who all wear jeans and broad belts! It is worth paying the price in order to belong. Now the young person can relax in the common protection of the uniform group.

Fashion designers know that need, and they literally live on it. They change the fashion every year so that last year's clothes will not do for this year, and there is the regular scramble for shoppers to find out which are this year's trends and adopt them with urgent haste. The passport has to be renewed, and the renewal costs money. Buy new clothes. Discard the old ones. Move with the group. Don't be left behind, don't be left alone. That is the final curse each one has to avoid. Therefore move ahead. Buy the latest fashion. Adopt it bravely. Learn how to pronounce with aplomb the latest vulgarity. That's the way. You are "in" again. It's a hard process, but it's worth the trouble. Be one of the crowd, even if the price you have to pay for it is not to be yourself any more.

G. K. Chesterton shrewdly observed the game some fifty years ago. This brief dialogue is from *The Vampire in the Village*: "The doctor: 'Well, you know I'm not particularly modern. I don't

enjoy this jazzing and joy-riding of the Bright Young Things.'—
'The Bright Young Things don't enjoy it,' said Father Brown.
'That is the real tragedy.' "* And George Mikes in *How to Be a
Guru* makes a similar observation: "A Hell's Angel (to choose
one type out of many) thinks he is a man who opts out; he, in
fact, is a man who opts in. He has failed, or he fears that he will
fail, in conventional society, and he has no doubt that it is
society's fault. So he tries an alternative society. He seeks to defy
conventional society, says he despises its rules and narrow outlook but, in fact, he is desperate for approval: the approval of a
sect. He does not shave half of his hair off and make a dirty mess
of the other half because he deems that hairstyle pretty. He has
to do it in order to gain the approval of those who hate doing it
just as much as he does but have to do it because, in turn, they
seek *his* approval. He may be a gentle soul, but he must go on the
rampage and bash in people's heads because this is the clan's
ritual. On such occasions, at least at the beginning, he does not
go wild and does not lose control, he simply follows a ritual, just
as offering a turn in a pub or singing the Red Flag is the ritual of
other gatherings. This is how many sects of non-believers are
created all over the world. Poor Hell's Angels! They are trying to
persuade themselves that they are strong individuals, defying
society; they are lonely babes crying out for mother's love."†

Society is cruel in its demand for conformity. Conform, and
thou shalt be saved; rebel, and thou shalt perish. That pressure
is felt by all, but especially by the young as they are more insecure and dependent. Maybe that was why Bertrand Russell said,
"The young are never real." The peer pressure to conform to
the group does not allow them to be. Though, in all honesty, I
have to give also the second part of Bertrand Russell's quotation
which makes me feel more uneasy because it applies to me. The

---

* G. K. Chesterton, *The Vampire in the Village*, in *The Penguin Complete Father Brown*,
Penguin Books, 1981, p. 706.
† George Mikes, *How to Be a Guru*, Penguin Books, 1986, p. 26.

full quotation is: "The young are never real. The unmarried very seldom." The unmarried often, as is my case, belong to a religious group, and again the pressure of the group can stifle the authenticity of the individual. The group offers security as a reward for curtailing one's individuality. That can be a high price to pay.

I once watched on TV some very brief interviews of young men and women as they were coming out of a four-hour outdoor rock concert, where they had stood in the thousands without chairs before a popular group of singers. Their faces were ecstatic, their bliss otherworldly, their vocabularies strained to their limits of expression. One of them summed up the glorious experience in these words: "It was wonderful to be one with a crowd of thousands who all felt the same and sang the same and moved together at the same time." A wonderful feeling. The security, if only for four hours, that all felt the same and did the same in the large crowd; that they were able to forget themselves, because all were one. A total uniformity achieved by the blending of thousands into one. The noise, the glare, the fatigue were all worthwhile if one could get lost in the many without any concern for his own private existence. All the insecurity of youth disappears for four hours in the guarantee of one feeling and one mood. A memory to cherish through the uncertainty of the daily struggle till another such occasion comes to redeem one's life from its burden of loneliness.

Most non-young people repeatedly proclaim that they cannot understand how the young enjoy such happenings, and that they themselves would not be able to stand even for five minutes in the blare and glare of a genuine hard-rock concert. I would not stand there myself, if only out of deference to my eardrums, but I fancy that I can to some extent understand why young people go and enjoy the din. They are relieved, for the time they are there, from the worry of being themselves, by surrendering to the unanimous beat of a mammoth crowd. They are given the chance to do what they most long to do in order to feel accepted, supported, secure: to conform. They all sway rhythmically, obliviously, obediently to the unquestioned lead of the acknowledged rock star. And they see that all do what they do, and they do what all do. They are there, they fit, they belong. And that is the deepest yearning of the wavering young heart.

While we talk of fashion and young people and their ways of dressing and singing, we feel safe and we see and comment without difficulty on how fashion has a conditioning effect on youth. The problem is that fashion applies not only to clothes and song but also to tasks and ideas, and not only to young people but to older workers and thinkers in every field where new ways of thinking and new things to be done appear and draw attention and promise reward. The reward of doing the latest thing and following the newest trend. Our minds are so much conditioned by what others around us say and do that it takes a strong conscious effort to achieve a certain degree of independence and neutrality. When we see young people follow the current, and we criticize their submissiveness to the group and their obedience to fashion, we shall do well to remember that we too are under such influences and that it is not easy for us to free ourselves from them. Who can afford to be truly original, different, creatively independent in today's routine world? The task is uphill, and therefore the challenge all the more appealing.

8

The Valley of the Blind

H. G. Wells adapted in story fashion an old legend preserved by the people of Peru. They tell the story of a group of their people who, fourteen generations ago, retreated to a close valley at a great altitude in the Andean Alps, where they lived by themselves cut off from the rest of civilization. Due to the effect of the great altitude and a contagious disease they gradually lost their sight till the whole group became totally blind. Their lives went on, however, as they developed their other senses and adapted to the situation. They could hear when someone approached, and recognize the person by the sound of his steps, and tell his moods, before he spoke, by the beat of his heart. They could find their way by the feel of the road, and could tell when the crops were ripe by the fragrance on the fields. They were a happy people.

Once, however, their happiness was threatened by an unexpected event. A chance explorer, lost in the Andes, happened upon the Valley of the Blind, and, seeking his own survival, established contact with them. The newcomer soon realized that he was the only sighted person there and decided to stay in order to help them, with his sight, to lead a better life. In the process he, of course, would become the leader of the group, as among the blind even the one-eyed man is a king. He had two eyes, and wanted to prove to them the advantage that gave him.

But, to his surprise, he could not convince them. He devised proofs, but they did not work. He asked them to surround him in a circle, and he would escape by walking stealthily through a gap between them; but their ears were exceedingly sharp and they closed ranks before he could get through. They outran him on the open fields, as their ears could pick their way faster than his eyes, and they could collect faster the fruit of the trees, as they sensed its ripeness by smell and touch with greater speed and accuracy than he could do by sight. In fact the experiment backfired, and, to the explorer's irritation, they came to consider him as a sick man, and his sightedness as a bodily defect that hindered the natural development of his senses. To them he was handicapped, and as such they treated him.

Meanwhile, he had fallen in love with a girl in the group. The girl was blind, of course, but he thought that once they were married he could take her back to civilization and medical treatment there could restore her sight. But things worked otherwise. When he asked the girl, she answered, "I also love you and want to marry you. There is, however, one difficulty. I have consulted the elders of our people, and they have no other problem except that, as you know, and pardon me for mentioning it but I hope you won't mind, you have an eye disease which has stunted you and your senses, and I don't mind personally, of course, but they worry that if you marry me your disease may spread among our people and we may all become infected and lose our health. Now, there is a remedy for that, and since you love me so much I do not doubt you will be ready for it. There are some very skilled surgeons among us, they will perform an operation on your eyes and they will become normal and then we can marry. The operation is not painful, and its result is guaranteed. You will then be like one of us, you will develop fully like a true human being, and we shall marry and be happy. They are ready to perform the operation tomorrow. For your sake and for mine, will you accept?"

The explorer thought throughout the night. He understood fully the import of the girl's words: They wanted to make him blind. The operation would be the removal of his eyes. They wanted to make him "normal," and normal for them meant blind as they all were. It almost made sense to the man who had seen how they functioned within their own limitations, and who was now deeply in love with the blind girl.

In the darkness of the night, where blindness and sight merge in a common shadow, he became ready for the sacrifice and accepted the test of his love. He would willingly become blind. But the early morning brought the first rays of the rising sun to play upon the myriad hues and colors of the enchanted valley. The beauty of its hills, its meadows, its river, its flowers awakened all at once with the irresistible charm of virgin nature at the break of day. The man looked in wonder, took in the full canvas of the fresh scenery, tried for a moment to say good-bye to it all, but found that he could not. He would not be blind. He woke up at last from the slumber of his romance, feeling desperate enough to foil this time the vigilance of the blind guards, and escaped into safety, into the world of life and color that was his own, far from the Valley of the Blind.

The story has a lesson. Mankind is blind. Not that people cannot manage and live somehow; they do feel their way through the paths of life and raise their crops and somehow fill their bellies. But they are blind. They miss the beauty and the color and the meaning of life and the faith in eternity and the blue of the sky and the green of the fields and the flowers and the birds. People are blind, and have adapted their ways of life to their blindness. Their thought and their behavior, their principles and their values are those of the blind. Legitimate in their situation, but limited by their lack of sight. There is no vision. The tragedy begins when one person in society opens his eyes and dares to see. He is a threat to society, because he sees what its other members do not see, he talks of things they do not understand, he does things they cannot imitate, he is different, he is strange, he is "diseased." His eyesight is a defect and the tumor has to be removed. Be like us, and all will be well with you. You'll be able to marry the girl you love, and to live happily ever after. You only have to pay a small price, and that is for your own good. A brief operation. Painless and safe. Close your eyes forever. Cease to see, cease to think, cease to be independent, cease to be yourself. Surrender your sight, your views, your freedom. Conform to the group. And the group will take you into the fold, will protect you, defend you, respect you, give you honor and safety. You will have nothing to worry about for the rest of your life. Only surrender your eyes. Sacrifice your vision. Give up your ideals. Subscribe to our creed and swear to our constitution, and you will be safe, honored, and happy. But do not dare to open your eyes again. If you do, you will feel the irresistible temptation to run away from the valley.

The theme seems to be a recurrent one in literary compositions, and I can think of a few, of quite different styles, times, and origins, which in one way or another employ a similar parable. *Jonathan Livingston Seagull* presents a gull that wants to fly higher and faster and farther than all the others, and meets with the criticism, opposition, cynicism of all the other gulls in the rocky shore. Older gulls will not countenance the adventurous exploits of the inexperienced winged youth in search of instant flight.

Flatland, a Romance in Many Dimensions depicts the misadventures of an enterprising triangle in a two-dimensional world, that guesses there is a third dimension, jumps upward into it, and returns to the original plane to tell an incredulous audience— composed of polygons and circles—about the wonders of the three-dimensional world of weight, volume, and perspective he has observed in space. The reaction is the standard one repeated in all these stories: First they dismiss him as mad, and then, as he persists in his story, they put him in jail as dangerous. No person is more dangerous than one who has seen the truth. He has to be silenced at all costs. First discredit him, and then imprison him. That happens to our enterprising triangle.

In *Logan's Run* the scene shifts to a science fiction background where people live in a bubble city with all comforts and full leisure, under the single accepted regulation of ending one's life at thirty in the painless carousel of death. Logan discovers that life need not end at thirty, finds in fact an old man living happily outside the city, and comes back with him and the good news to liberate his fellow citizens. They are amused at his story, they laugh at him, they dismiss his tale, and when he, in his zeal, turns emotional and begins to harangue the crowds, the state police try to hold him and kill him, but, in this case, he escapes and liberates the city.

The Ugly Duckling is the charming tale of a swan's egg hatched among duckling eggs, with the subsequent efforts of the mother duck to make the unshapely specimen conform to what a proper duck should look like and do. *The Emperor's Clothes* emphasizes the nonconformity of a spontaneous child in the midst of a unanimous conspiracy of social lies. And even *The Little Prince* brings us a lovely visitor from a little planet, who finds it very difficult to understand the ways of a businessman who buys more stars in order to have more money in order to buy more stars in order to have more money . . . ; of the lamp-lighter who keeps switching a lamp on and off to nobody's benefit in fulfillment of an obsolete order; of the king who rules over nonexistent subjects; till he, the prince, has to die an inevitable death to escape from this planet in which there is no place for him. Always the story of a humdrum society where anybody who does not conform is a misfit and has to be gotten rid of. The story of the little prince has echoes from the gospel in the pathetic premonition of his innocent death. Jesus did not fit in his society either.

9

Laugh When You Are Told

The following experiment has been performed with different people and similar results. Twenty-five people are gathered in a room with the instruction to watch the pictures that appear on a screen in front of them, and decide which of two objects shown at a time is bigger or taller or longer than the other. A simple task, to all appearances. The catch is that twenty of those people have been instructed to say, when the objects appear on the screen and comments are allowed before judgment is passed, that the bigger object is in fact the smaller one, while the other five are innocent of the plot and are to judge freely according to what they see. Two lines are projected on the screen, of which line A is obviously longer than line B. When comments start, however, the twenty people who have been instructed to do so all begin to say, each in his or her own way, that B is actually longer than A. They have practiced their remarks, so that they sound quite effective and convincing. This makes the five independent people begin to have doubts. Our eyes seem to see otherwise, but, no, in spite of all appearances B is definitely longer than A. When everybody agrees on a point, who am I to venture a different opinion? Yes, yes, there is no doubt. It is clear now. Good that I have listened to the others before venturing on my own opinion. Nobody wants to risk making a fool of himself, and so for safety's sake they all follow the majority and join the common verdict. When the open vote is taken and the twenty people begin to declare B longer than A, it is found that the other five people too follow suit and pronounce B longer than A, even against their best judgment. The pressure of the group prevails against the personal conviction of the individual.

What will happen when not twenty people but the whole society, and not for one session but for the whole lifetime, keep repeating that B is longer than A? And what will happen when there is not just a question of straight lines whose length can be accurately measured and compared, but of ideas and opinions that can be shaped in many ways and viewed from different angles? Personal evidence is then much more questionable, and can be easily abandoned for a safer common opinion. When the whole world says one thing, it is very difficult for the individual person to say another.

Some comic TV serials use a simple device to make sure the viewers laugh at the proper time and nobody misses the fact that the program is indeed funny. Whenever a character on the screen says something the producers consider funny, some background laughter is provided by an unseen group of professional "laughers" who let out a burst of laughter at the exact time and for the exact duration required by the witticism. Maybe only two characters appear on the screen, but the anonymous cheerers are hidden somewhere and perform their cheerful duty with unfailing precision. One does suspect that the laughter comes only from a tape someone sets in motion by pressing a key while the dialogue is going on, but the effect in any case is clear, and its purpose unmistakable. It tells the viewers when to laugh.

I was once watching such a program together with a few other people. The program was British, but the people were not, and some indeed experienced a slight difficulty in following the niceties of the dialogue. It was then that I understood the usefulness of the device. It told people when to laugh, even when they had missed the joke. That was a great help in saving face. Nobody wanted, by missing a joke and failing to laugh at the appropriate time, to give away the fact that he or she did not master the English language or could not follow the subtleties of British humor. That is where the background laughter proved so useful. All one had to do was pay attention to each initial burst, and laugh at once on cue. The system worked to everybody's satisfaction. All laughed at the required moments and for the exact length of time. Only occasionally an eager viewer would make a false start or prolong his contribution beyond the official time. Such a faux pas was silently frowned upon by the rest, and punctuated by a marked silence to expose his discomfiture. But by and large the method proved successful. The safety of the regulated laughter allowed everybody to watch the program with an easy conscience. One can only hope TV technicians find a similar device for tragic programs to tell us when to weep, and then we shall be able to watch TV without a care on our soul. We will follow the signals and weep when we are told to weep and laugh when told to laugh. The "wise box" will then rule our lives more effectively, not only by telling us what we may view but by prompting the appropriate reaction at exactly the proper time. The ultimate convenience.

I am allowing myself a gentle satire on modern society and its submissive ways. I see a symbol and figure of the workings of modern society in another machine that has become indispensable for the running of our lives today: the Xerox machine. A machine to make copies. Fast and exact. A compulsory ornament in any office. Or, if we cannot afford to own one, an available facility at the nearest copy shop. Only a few years ago the contraption was unknown among us. A copy meant a carbon paper into the typewriter, or a laboriously run stencil in a cumbersome duplicator. Now in our neighborhood alone there are eight Xerox shops that offer instant copies at competitive prices. And they are always full of customers. In and out. Hand over the original and name the number of copies. The more copies you order, the cheaper they come. Make more in case you need them. Full service. The copies look even better than the original. And today's society requires copies of everything: documents, originals, minutes, records, manuscripts, accounts. Everything has to be copied, multiplied, distributed, preserved. We live in a world of red tape, and the Xerox machine is the symbol and instrument of the new civilization. The essence of red tape is to make us all conform to a pattern. The file, the norm, the precedent. Do today as it was done yesterday. In other words, copy the past. Get your life from the Xerox machine. It is cheap and neat. Repetition is salvation. And the outcome is guaranteed: The man in the Xerox shop will immediately make another copy free of charge if the first is not satisfactory.

Many of our beliefs are Xerox beliefs. Much of our behavior is Xerox behavior. Most of our teaching is Xerox teaching. Faithful reproduction. If the student cribs in the examination using an unpermitted summary in his pocket, he is penalized when caught. If he copies in his mind from the memorized page, he is rewarded with a high grade. Yet the essential process is the same in both cases: transfer from one page to another. This goes beyond words, too. Original masterpieces of art hang in the museums of the world. All that we have in our hands is copies, and copies of copies. Xerox is now available in color too.

As computers invade one field after another in public (and now private) life, human existence will become more and more regimented. Computers are machines, and machines are repetitive. Whoever conforms to that repetition will find grace with the machine, and will be blessed in a world largely run by machines. And so people will conform more and more to set patterns and proven ways. Safety and comfort lie in those ways. Humanity is in for an age of stereotypes. Robots will liberate human beings from tiresome chores, but they will exact a price. To adapt to a factory—and eventually to a home—that is run by robots, one has to become a bit of a robot oneself. That is the immediate danger that threatens the progress of mankind. Loss of independence in a mechanized world.

The hope and the challenge is that, in a routinized universe, living individuals will be motivated to escape the common curse by creative adventure. The adventurers of the past explored virgin lands and remote mountain peaks; those of the future will explore with greater risk and deeper thrills the virgin lands of personality and originality, and the lonely peaks of independent existence. There will always be people who, in the midst of a standardized world, will seek the personal expression of a different life. Those will be the prophets of the future.

10

New Wineskins

Special tact is required in applying to one's religious experience the principle of freedom from the past which I am advocating here. While it is true that our religious experience is conditioned by the time, place, and family we are born in, it is equally true that God's will for me has been manifested through those circumstances, and in consequence I cannot be indifferent to my first training and upbringing. The broad guideline I have indicated in a general context applies also here. Freedom from the past does not in any way mean disowning one's past or rejecting it; it means screening in responsibility and freedom my present ideas to discern in full sincerity which ones have become truly mine through personal conviction and genuine internalization, and which have remained external, artificial, imposed. In religion also we have to distinguish the essential message from the accidental modes it has acquired in transmission. Even within the same religion and within the same branch of a religion, usages change and expressions of belief are refined throughout the ages; this purifying process takes place in the religious institution over the course of centuries, and in the growing individual over the course of a lifetime. This growth is welcome, and helps the person to understand better and live more deeply his or her own religious convictions.

Such a process, however, is not an easy one, and the corresponding attitude is not easily adopted. The fear of departing from tradition, and the urge to ensure continuity, often prompt the devout person to repeat rituals and stick to accepted usage, seeking safety in repetition rather than progress in innovation. Religious institutions are rightly cautious when it comes to accepting changes, and some people in them look to the past more often than the future. Prophets usually have a hard time among religious people, while traditional preachers are listened to with pleasure and honored with gratitude.

A concrete phenomenon that, in its extreme manifestations, can help us to realize the dangers of organized belief as practiced by well-intentioned but not always well-advised people, is the emergence of religious sects of all denominations in all parts of the globe. The present proliferation of religious sects in both East and West is a serious cause of worry for people concerned with true religious values. In those sects allegiance to a teacher is prized above all other virtues, and at times the disciple's intellectual independence is sacrificed to a misunderstood and abused loyalty. This tendency, carried to extremes in members of a sect, can also be present in a milder way in other people of piously inclined mentality; this can at times create difficulties in their intimate growth and integration. Religious circles are predominantly conservative, and an excessively rigid interpretation of common doctrines may on occasion lead to stagnation in the development of a person's ideas and practices.

Father Daniel A. Helminiak in his interdisciplinary study on *Spiritual Development* states that "spiritual development first becomes possible when one begins to move out of the Conformist Stage" which he defines as that of a coherent, rational, borrowed, external-authority-supported ideology embedded in the world of family and peers, school and work. "But that movement is difficult and precarious," he continues. "Many people never completely transcend the Conformist Stage to achieve the Conscientious Stage characterized by complete personal internalization of rules and ideas. Rather, they remain in the half-way station . . . and become, in Loevinger's all too accurate formulation, conscientiously conformist. So for most people spiritual development quickly becomes a moot issue. Unfortunately, that comment often applies even to people committed professionally to religious pursuit and to others whose well-publicized avocation is interest in spirituality or whose recent 'charismatic' conversion experience has brought new meaning and religious affiliation. Inspired by stories of the 'saints,' by models of 'holiness' or 'enlightenment,' or by accounts of miraculous occurrences, they become but faithful imitators. Too intent on becoming 'spiritual,' they follow the master, keep the rules, affirm the teachings, all without question or responsible criticism. Good will is turned into slavery, often to the advantage of some sponsoring institution: almost no institution can afford to encourage people to grow and to think, to make decisions for themselves. So people 'authentically realize unauthenticity.' They become skilled in the virtue of the child, obedience, and never experience the adult phenomenon, spiritual development."*

Spiritual development is important not only for the individual but for society and for religion itself. If we want religion to thrive and flourish in our day with new vigor and renewed life, we must encourage personal reflection and adult awareness in religious faith and practice. This will benefit not only the person but the religious society to which the person belongs, by the contributions made to the common growth through his or her own personal efforts. The fact is, however, that even sincerely religious people can adopt the narrow attitude of insisting on norms and rituals which are meaningful to them but not necessarily so to others, and this insistence may cause tensions in the religious community and disaffection in some of its members. In that case it is wisest to keep loyally to one's own ways while refraining

* Daniel A. Helminiak, *Spiritual Development*, Loyola University Press, 1987, p. 78.

from imposing them on others. Here is an amusing example from my own experience.

A sincere leader of a flourishing sect in a non-Christian religion called me aside after a lecture of mine in his institution, and, when we were alone, he looked intensely and lovingly into my eyes and said to me with his soul in every word: "I have read your books and watched your life for some time now, and today I have listened with great interest to your thoughts and experiences in your talk. All that you have said and stand for meets with my full approval. I believe that God is in you, and that you are an enlightened person. But there is one thing still lacking in you for full enlightenment, and, precisely because I appreciate you and trust you, I feel moved by the Lord to propose it to you. I have experienced in my life in an unmistakable way the power and joy that have come to me through the blessings of my own guru, and I know that if that blessing and that power would come to you, your life and your work would acquire an entirely new depth and dimension, and you would be able to reach far more people in a far more effective way for their good and for the glory of God on earth. Now, all you have to do for that is to recite after me the sacred formula I will pronounce, and bow at the name of the guru, and wear always round your neck this locket with his picture. Nobody need know about it, and I for my part will not say a word to anyone. I am not doing this for any sordid gain or as a proselytizing gimmick, but for your own good and the good of all those you reach with your writings and your talks. Think of the spiritual benefits they will reap if you take this step which I firmly believe is God's will for you. Are you ready to do it for their sake?"

I respected the man's conviction and zeal, and spoke gently in my answer. He meant well and was convinced he was doing the right thing in asking me to follow his guru. It was also true that I am by no means perfect and many things are lacking in me. But one thing I certainly do not need is the repeating of a formula or

bowing or wearing the picture of a strange guru around my neck.
I can well do without that. I told the man that I appreciated his
gesture, which for him was the greatest sign of appreciation he
could give, and that I myself had felt in my life the fervor and
the bliss given to me by my faith in the Lord Jesus, and I knew in
my soul the sacred urge to share with others what meant so
much to me. I said that for this very reason I would not submit
to the ritual, and that, if he had done the right thing before his
conscience in asking me, I was doing the right thing before mine
in refusing. He would respect my convictions, I hoped, as I respected his. His disappointment showed in his silence. For my
part I was conscious of a suppressed feeling of anger, not at his
desire to enrich my spiritual life with his, but at the mention of
the formula and the picture. If he had told me that he wanted
me to know his religion better, and had given me books or
proposed a dialogue, I would have gratefully accepted the offer
and would have opened my mind without fear to the new experience. But all he wanted was to have me repeat an incantation
and wear a talisman. And he was a holy man in his religion, an
honored teacher and a respected authority! If this is all religion
has to offer, I thought, no wonder we are in crisis, and indifference grows all around us. Repeat the words and tie carefully the
thread. That is all you need. Follow my guru and you are safe.
Bow your head. Surrender your mind. Someone else has done all
the thinking for you, and all you need now is to repeat what you
are told. If that is enlightenment, there is not much light in it,
and if that is religion, it is a very sorry religion.

The little episode, which in itself had been more comic than
serious, left me with a sad aftertaste. If men of religion institu-
tionalize their practices to such a degree, little life will be left in
their religion. In the interest, therefore, of religious faith and
observance it is urgent that we practice our religion not only
with our heart but also with our mind, not only with fidelity to

the past but also with imagination for the future. The world needs religious faith, and religious faith needs the generous commitment of modern men and women to live it in ways consonant with our age. New wine in new wineskins.

11

Image of Clay

The greatest conditioners are not our parents or our teachers, not society or the environment, but we ourselves. Each one for himself or herself. I for myself. That is, my past conditions my present. And let me make it clear from the beginning that my past is fine and welcome and necessary, it is happily and intimately part of me and it will always remain so. The danger is when the past becomes the rule for the present, and past memories stifle present realities.

Life is made up of habits, and soon in our worldly career we acquire an image that accompanies us for the rest of our lives as our visiting card, our introduction, our biodata. People come to know my habits, and soon they brand me as an unfailingly punctual person who will never arrive a minute late, or, on the contrary, as a hopelessly unreliable tramp who will never keep an appointment or turn up at the appointed time. And punctuality is only an example. The same applies to my ways of thinking and acting, to my weaknesses and my genialities. My acquaintances have drawn a fairly accurate picture of me as I appear and behave in their presence, and they use it to identify me and foretell my behavior on a given occasion: Oh, that's him; yes, he *would* do that.

The point here is not that others have this image of me, but that I *myself* have it, and this image I have of myself conditions my way of acting on subsequent occasions. I know myself as a punctual person, and so I make it a point to arrive at the exact time to conform to expectations, and, more than that, not to fail myself in my private expectation of my future behavior. Now let us analyze that situation with a little detail. Punctuality in itself is a good thing (or so I believe), and so can be even the habit of being punctual. What is not so good is the compulsive need to be punctual because I have always been and if I fail to be now I shall feel I have betrayed my own self, broken my image, ceased to be me. That is bondage. That is idolatrous worship of a clay image. That is loss of freedom under the inner rigidity of conformity to a set pattern. If I arrive punctually because I freely and cheerfully want to do so, because I am sensitive to the convenience of others and responsible in the use of my time, that is fine and healthy; but if I keep my time because I cannot do otherwise, because I shall feel guilty and lost if I miss it by only five minutes, because I need to be in time in order to be myself and feel secure, then my punctuality is no ornament of character but the sorry expression of an insecure mind.

A good image provides safety and respectability, and that is why we cling to it. But (and the idea is coming up for the third or fourth time in these pages) safety is secured only at the expense of openness, spontaneity, and freedom. It is threatening to break one's image, because it is like going out of one's home, one's land, one's familiar surroundings. It is throwing away crutches and breaking molds. Hard to do. But the chicken will not grow unless it breaks the shell. To put aside, gently and lovingly, one's image—if only for a while—can be an exercise in courage and growth. One may not like to return to it after that.

So far I have been speaking of a good image. Even that may be enslaving and therefore worth breaking. But this is all the more true of a negative image. Under it the slavery is twofold, to the image as such and to what it makes the victim do. A bit of holy iconoclasm can be definitely called for here. I knew a man who was notorious in his company for always telling new jokes, not precisely of the cleanest kind. Whenever he appeared, he was asked by the people who knew him and his reputation: "Tell us the latest one!" And he had to comply. His image had preceded him. He came to be disgusted with it himself, and wanted to get rid of his unhappy fame, but could not. People were adamant. He was known for that unholy charisma, and had to live up to it whether he wanted it or not. He told his latest joke. People laughed outwardly. He sulked inwardly. Society can be cruel. I may be mistaken, but I do not think people were interested in his jokes; rather, they were interested in keeping him in the behavioral prison he had built for himself. It can take great courage and determination to break an image that years have built. It can take courage to refuse to tell a dirty joke.

At first sight it might seem that personal experience, as against outside authority, is a genuine source of a free personality and an independent character. Indeed it is, but there is a catch in it too. When I accept an idea or come to appreciate a practice through my own personal experience, rather than through an external injunction, I act out of conviction, and such an idea or practice then takes on a deeper value to me and expresses a more personal commitment. This is very valid, and emphasizes the importance of experiencing things by oneself rather than accepting them blindly from another. But, I say, there is a catch in it. My past experience, however valid at the time, may now become an "authority" for me, as foreign to the present me as an outside source at any time. My old ideas, convictions, values, experiences were genuine at the time they happened; they form part of my being and have shaped my life; but if they become rigid norms to make me act today as I understood yesterday, they are no better than an external power acting on me. They are external to me in time, if not in space—that is, they do not come from outside, but they come from the past, and as such they are foreign matter and dead weight.

"You had an experience yesterday which taught you something, and what it taught you becomes a new authority—and
that authority of yesterday is as destructive as the authority of a
thousand years," Krishnamurti tells us. This is a difficult lesson
to learn. Our experiences are so precious to us that we treasure
them as valid forever, and consider it a loss and a betrayal to
abandon them. We say to ourselves, I have seen it, felt it, experienced it, how can I now let it go, disown it, forget it? My experience is what marks my life as mine, and therefore I must keep it
for life, vivid and fresh as when it happened to me. Such is our
reaction, and it is fully understandable. It is also futile. That
experience was a fresh flower when it first happened, but no
amount of watering and gardening can keep that flower fresh
forever. The flower fades and withers and dies. A concrete experience was meant for a concrete time, and as it was allowed to
come when it happened so it must be let go when it recedes.
Make room for life. Clean the garden. Drop the old flowers to
gather new ones. A past experience converted into present authority is all the more damaging because it comes from ourselves
and so we are more ready to submit to it. And yet Krishnamurti's words are true: "The authority of yesterday is as destructive
as the authority of a thousand years." The authority of my own
past is as destructive as the authority of a thousand teachers. It
prevents me from opening myself to new experiences in order to
follow my life, to keep on breathing. I must free myself even
from myself if I want to advance along the path of life and find
new horizons and climb new heights. Of little use will my freedom from others be if I do not free myself from myself. This is
the most subtle and dangerous trap because it is within me and
is part of me. I am to keep myself ready, alert, growing, understanding that today's garland is tomorrow's chain, and yesterday's glorious experience is today's honored but buried past.

This is the moment to repeat that my present norms of conduct and belief are not to be rejected simply because they come

from the past or they come from outside. The true view is to take myself as I am now, and see in responsibility and freedom which of those norms fit in with me as I know and want myself to be, and which of those norms are artificial or dated and no longer make any sense to me in my present state; which ones have become living tissue in my flesh and blood through inner conviction, practice, and assimilation, and which ones are only transitory feelings that did their job in their time and can now be gently and gratefully dismissed to make room for new experiences and new growth. This is the way every healthy organism functions.

We not only have our own image, but we try to project it onto others and exhort them to follow what we follow and do as we do, as nothing will give us more security that to see others follow our own way of life. As we grow older we instinctively preach to others and try to influence them and bend them toward our direction. This effort to convince others may or may not succeed with them, but in any case it does succeed with ourselves—that is, it succeeds in making us even stronger and firmer in our own ideas and practices. By trying to convince others we finally succeed in convincing ourselves.

An ancient tale has it that one day Mulla Nasruddin was being harassed by children in the village who abused him and started throwing stones at him. As the children were many and he was not strong, he had to think quickly to find a way out. He suddenly struck on an idea and told the children, "Do you know what day is today?" They answered, "No, and we don't care, because you only want to get rid of us with some of your tricks." He said, "Trick or no trick, today is the king's birthday, and he gives food and sweets free to anyone who goes to the palace." Then he began to describe the food and the sweets with such detail that the children started off at full speed for the royal palace. The Mulla saw them disappear around the corner of the street, when he suddenly checked himself, hurriedly took his tunic and started running in the same direction. "I'd better go and see for myself," he murmured as he ran, "maybe there is some truth in it after all." The fervor of his own description had carried him off with the rest.

II

TAMING
THE
FUTURE

12

When Can We Begin to Play?

Strangely enough, it is not only our past that conditions us but our future as well. If we have an image of what we have been, and that past image presides over our present behavior, so we have also an image of what we should like to be, and that future image also inspires and directs our present efforts. Most of the time we are all striving to be something different from what we are. And because we are so consistently endeavoring to be what we are not, we thereby miss in fact what we actually are. We make plans for the future which do not allow us to see the present, and think of later improvements which prevent us from seeing and enjoying the good we already have now. Again, there is nothing at all wrong with planning, proposing, resolving, dreaming; but if the planning and the dreaming make us lose contact with the present reality, we shall be neither here nor there—present in body where we are not in mind, and absent in mind from where we are present in body. The result will be a life of absences under cover of dreams. A ghost existence. The burden of the future can be as heavy as the burden of the past.

Most of us are to some extent dissatisfied with what we are, aware that we could be better, and determined to be so at a more or less remote future. Nothing is wrong with wanting to improve; however, if the resolve to do better in the future shields us from the duty to do well now, we shall find that at the moment of acting (that is, now) we lack the motivation to do our best, as this best will come only at an indeterminate future date —and whatever energies we have are concentrated on that uncertain future date, leaving unassisted the present which, devoid of those energies, can only drag along in minimal existence. This explains the low level of vitality at which we usually function; we keep our evident strength for a future which never comes, and make do meanwhile with a routine performance which satisfies nobody, least of all ourselves. If we could learn to use the fullness of our possibilities at every point of time in our busy lives, we would be surprised at the tide of joy of heart and zest for work that would sweep through our enlarged horizons. We are spread out thin over past and future. It is time we regain the conscience of our present and return to the perennial source of youth which is the contact, at once committed and detached, with all that happens at the time it happens. This is the secret of life.

We live under the sign of the future. The child dreams of growing up, the student of graduating, the graduate of getting employment, the employed of getting married, the married of having children and seeing them grow up and get married in turn—and we all dream of a future life in which we shall be happy forever in the company of the saints. Our sights are always on the future. Something new is due to come into our lives after each turn in the long way, and it is the hope and longing for that new event that keeps us going till we reach it and begin to think of the next one to come. One's whole life is a series of partial fulfillments, and the point is that while we are in one stage we consistently believe that the truly blissful and definitive stage will be the new one—only to transfer the bliss to the next one when this one is reached. Thus we miss the beauty and the enjoyment of each stage by dwelling all the time on the beauty and enjoyment of the next in line. The imagined glory of tomorrow casts a gloom over the present reality of today. We do not recognize what we have because we expect to be given something better. We keep missing the blessings we receive by thinking of those that are still to come. It is high time we start enjoying life instead of waiting for the next enjoyment.

When Mulla Nasruddin reached his fifth birthday his mother organized a big party for him and his friends. There were party hats and balloons, whistles and sticks, sweets and drinks, and all kinds of games to play in twos or threes or for the whole group together with music and toys. A perfect feast. At the height of it all, little Nasruddin went to where his mother was standing, in charge of all the arrangements and feeling pride in the successful party, and asked her plaintively: "Mummy, when all this is over, can we go out and play?"

To me there is immense pathos in that innocent story. The party is on, and the child is waiting for it to be over in order to play. Let us not argue that the games at a party are artificial and organized, while the child wants his own daily unprogrammed romping. That may be true, but it is not the point of the story. In the story the party is fine, and the games played at it are infinitely more amusing and entertaining than the daily fare of the children in the street. But the child does not see it. He does not see the fun and the wit and the art and the joy of the birthday party, and is thinking only of when it will be over and the real fun will begin. At that rate the real fun never begins.

God has organized for us a lovely party down here on earth, with food and music and dances and games, and a beautiful setting he has made for us all to enjoy. And we, in the midst of it, muse and ponder when real life will be given to us so that we can begin to enjoy it. When all this is over shall we be allowed to go out and play?

When all this is over. But is not "all this" also God's gift and God's game? This is God's party right enough, and we are missing its laughter and gaiety. The game of life, which is the supreme game of creation, is going on before our very eyes, and we are bored and annoyed because we are waiting for another game.

Some time, somewhere we shall be able to go out and play. But what of the present? What of today's party? What of this hour? What of this day? We think only of when this will be over. Only to think again, as soon as the next item begins, when that will be over in turn. Each day is passed in the expectation of its getting finished. Whatever we are doing, the one longing of our heart is: When will this be over? When will this day come to an end? When will the next day begin so that we can begin to pray for it to end? A succession of empty expectations. A repetition of birthday parties. A succession of birthdays. A succession of days. Each a preparation for the next one, and so not a single one valid in itself. Each as grey as the one that preceded it, because its function is only to point to the one that will follow. A row of ciphers without the one that would redeem their emptiness. And they call that "life." No wonder the question comes up now with greater strength and urgency about the whole of that life: When will it be over? If it is only a succession of empty spaces, we cannot do very much more about it than wait patiently for it to end.

Once I went to the city of Jamnagar in Gujarat for a speaking engagement. There was a young man in that city who had corresponded with me and who, on learning that I was going to that place, urged me to visit his house as his family would be glad to meet me. I agreed, and asked the organizers of my trip to find half an hour in the day's schedule for me to visit that home. So it was arranged, and so I went after informing him of the time. He was waiting for me outside the house, and when I got down from the car and faced him, his very first words to me were, "The next time you come to my house, you must stay a full day with us." That was his greeting to me. And I took time to explain to him, and to all those who had gathered at his house and were ready to listen, my own spontaneous reaction to his greeting: "I have not yet set foot in your house for the first time, and you are telling me what to do when I come next time. God knows when I shall come again to this city and to this house, but today I have come and I am happy to have come and am ready to have a pleasant—though short—time with you and your family if only you allow me to do so. You find short the time we are going to spend together today, and you begin by complaining about it and want to make sure now that the next time will be longer. I do appreciate that and love you for that. But I am afraid that by trying to ensure a future meeting you are effectively going to ruin the present one. You seem ready to spend this half hour deciding with me how many hours I have to stay when I come next time. Those hours may never come, and this half hour is not going to be a very happy event if you follow that course. I have had a busy time today in your city, I was happy and proud of myself that I had remembered your request and had been able to accommodate it. I was looking forward to meeting you and your family, I wanted to be introduced to them, learn their names and faces, take tea together (which I smell getting ready), chat and smile and relax and enjoy your company. Half an hour may not be a long time, but it is half an hour, and it could be a happy time if we make the most of it. Let us enjoy the meeting today as it is, and not spoil it thinking of the ideal meeting which may never take place." We finally sat down. He introduced me to all. I looked at their faces and learned their names. We all took our tea together and after half an hour I got up. He then brought me his autograph album and asked me to sign it. I wrote: "Do not miss the present by dreaming of the future." He understood.

13

How to Catch a Bus

The worries of the future often rob us of the enjoyment of the present. That is, the imagining of what is going to happen tomorrow prevents us from being fully ourselves today. And, in a similar but no less effective way, the anticipation of the good things that are due to befall us later on diminishes our ability to draw full advantage from the good things we could be enjoying at this moment. The image of what I could be in a more or less distant future dims the reality of what I am now. To be fully myself I have to learn to be fully now.

This in no way invalidates the importance of foreseeing the future and planning for it. Just as the past is important in our memory and as the history and foundation of whatever comes after it, so the future, and therefore the thought of it, is indispensable in directing our lives along the lines we want them to proceed. The danger comes when the planning outgrows the living, and the dream overshadows the reality. The wisdom lies in revitalizing the present with the gentle vision of the future.

A comparison: A good driver is driving a reliable car. He keeps his eyes on the road in front of him and on the traffic, the car ahead, the traffic lights, the side roads; he casts a look at the distance to take in the faraway scene, and gives simultaneous attention to the rear mirror to be conscious of what comes in from behind. That is, he has an all-around awareness with his most immediate concrete attention on the situation just in front, while ready to react quickly to any emergency in his steady course. If he starts looking at the beautiful landscape in the distance, to turn his head sideways to enjoy the sight, to turn bodily and look back while driving . . . he is inviting an accident. The present can be turned into a tragic experience if the past and the future are allowed to rule one's life.

Once I was an unwilling witness to such an accident. I was being driven in a car through a busy street in a crowded Indian city, sitting in front by the side of the driver while two more people sat at the back in lively conversation. Then it happened, and I saw it all in a flash. The driver turned his head for a moment to say something to the man behind him; in the same instant a pedestrian on the left side of the road saw a bus as it reached and stopped at the bus-stand on the right of the road, and without looking to his right or left made a dash across the road for the bus. His trajectory crossed with that of our car. Neither he, who was looking ahead, nor the driver who was looking back, saw or noticed each other, and we collided. I felt physically the impact of the man's body against our car, saw the look of anguished surprise in his eyes at the sudden shock, suffered when I heard him, already in a hospital bed, curse his bad luck and tell of the hardships he and his family would have to endure till the several fractures he had suffered would heal. That was no moment for philosophizing, but the memory of the unhappy incident did remain in my mind as a vivid image of the mishap brought about by a man who looked forward and a man who looked backward. If either of the two had looked in front of him, the accident would have been avoided.

A man who is running to catch a bus is a striking image of the mental distortion we suffer when we dream of the future to the detriment of the present. There he is intent on being where he is not, and failing to be where he is. His whole mind, his desire, his outstretched hand focus on that fleeting point in space where he longs to be, while he has lost all contact with where he is, with all reality, all ground. He has lost *himself* in the effort to be where he is not. He is a man-on-the-street and wants to be a man-in-the-bus; and he is neither. He is not on the street because he does not realize it any more, and he is not in the bus which he has not boarded yet. He is stretched between two points in space, and belongs to neither. A man who belongs nowhere is not himself; and a man who is not himself is nothing. He misses the only reality which could be his at the time, and if he goes on living like that he will find at the end of his life that he has hardly lived.

Compare the man's desperate dash for the bus with the measured step of a man who runs for pleasure. Maybe the speed is the same, the step is the same, the way is the same, but in the runner's mind there is all the difference in the world. The man who runs for pleasure feels his body, fills his lungs, welcomes the touch of the breeze on his open face with rhythm and joy, whereas the man who runs to catch a bus is oblivious of everything except that red monster of a bus that threatens to depart without him. The beauty of life comes when we have learned so well how to run for pleasure that, when we have to run out of need, as in catching a bus, we can do so in the spirit of the game —with awareness of our surroundings, with joy in our feet, with fun in our haste, and with the sense of humor to laugh at ourselves when the bus departs unheedingly without us. In that spirit, as we go through all the labor and troubles and routines of this life, we will always have the outward smile and the inward leisure that enable us to connect with reality and enjoy every moment even in the midst of the continuous hustle. Learning how to run with a light heart and a simple mind, knowing that to miss a bus occasionally is no irreparable disaster—that is the way to avoid accidents.

Archbishop Bloom makes a telling comparison. A man is traveling in a train, and, in his haste to arrive at his destination earlier, he starts running inside the train from the last car right up to the engine through corridors, people, and luggage. People who see him will think he is out of his mind, and they will not be far wrong. He gains nothing by his senseless hurry; the train will arrive all of a piece at the same time and the doors will open together, leaving the engine farthest away along the platform with no gain for the runner. He will not arrive any earlier than the rest of the travelers, and only one thing is definite: He will have ruined his trip. Let him sit relaxedly near a window, enjoy the landscape, watch the fields and the trees and the cattle and the little buildings and the passing clouds; let him sense the thrill of speed, the adventure of being a moving speck in a steady world, the happy feeling of being free of moorings for a while between stations—without a home, without an address, without any of the constants that fix us down to a spot on earth and routinize our life. Blessed journey if he knows how to make the best of it, leaving it to be what it is: a journey. And life is a journey. Let us sit down in peace and enjoy the landscape.

S. I. Hayakawa gives another example which we all have experienced and endured. The elevator. A busy executive has entered the elevator, briefcase under his arm, and has pressed the button for the tenth floor. He looks at his watch, counting the minutes needed to be exactly in time for his all-important appointment. Then two small children also enter the elevator with the look of anticipated enjoyment in their eyes. They look at each other, glance at the double row of glaring buttons, and, to the executive's despair, one child presses a button and the other then presses several buttons in turn. They are going to have a ride and they mean to make the most of it. The elevator starts on its upward journey, stops at number three; the door opens, nobody goes out and nobody comes in, but the children look with delight at the whole process and then up at the row of buttons to guess when the next stop will come. The door closes and the trip continues. The executive suffers. For him the elevator is only an instrument to get to the tenth floor as fast as possible. His mind is on the tenth floor, his whole being is intent on getting there, he counts the seconds, he chafes at each stop, he is obviously not enjoying the trip. But the children are. For them it is a lift, a toy, an enjoyable experience for its own sake. They will actually regret reaching their destination, and, if the dour executive did not freeze them with a murderous look, they might continue up and down pressing buttons and seeing doors open and seeing them close till they declare the game over, drop the toy and begin another game. For the children the trip in the elevator is an end in itself, a lovely game, an experience to be enjoyed for its own sake, and they proceed to do so. For the executive it is only a means, efficient though irritating, to get to the tenth floor. He is thinking of the future, while the children are immersed in the present. He is going somewhere, while the children are staying. He is tense, while the children are absolutely relaxed. Too much so, indeed, for the executive's taste. He frets and looks at his watch. When will the tenth floor come and the door open for him to dash out to the office that is waiting for him? He will arrive there all worked up and annoyed and most likely will make a mess of whatever he is going to do there. He will be impatient in his office as he was impatient in the elevator, thinking of the next assignment on his timetable and looking at his watch and cursing all the people around who take life easy and seem to enjoy what they are doing without a worry for what is coming next. A man in a hurry is always a man in a hurry.

Life is for most of us what the elevator is for the executive: a means to get somewhere. And consequently we miss the fun of the experience. We think only of the tenth floor, of our future, of the end of our journey whatever that may be. We look at our watches, we count the years we have already lived and secretly conjecture how many more are left for us, and we want to make sure we arrive at the proper place at the proper time. The elevator ride as such has no attraction for us. Life in itself is unimportant. Its only value lies in being a stage for something else. We have no eyes for its beauty, no ears for its music. We know only how to press buttons to get things going and to get doors opened and doors closed. No wonder life is dull and existence drags on. The children are wiser in their spontaneous wonder, with their eyes open and their ears ready for any situation, experience, or object—even the four walls of a dreary elevator.

And now another experience, this time my own. I watched with an ill-repressed chuckle in a railway station in India as a wedding party was getting ready to board a train on their way to the ceremony. The wedding always takes place in the home of the bride, which more often than not is in a different city, and so the bridegroom with his family, relatives, and close friends set out in a body for the distant place, by bus if it is close and by train if it is far. This time about a hundred men and women in the colors and jewelry demanded by the occasion had booked an entire carriage for themselves, and the carriage was to be attached to a train which, being a slow train, would take eight hours to get them to their destination. Some technical difficulty arose at the last moment, and they were informed, when already on the platform, that their special carriage would be attached instead to a fast train that would cover the same distance in half the time, about four hours. In the West this would have been considered an advantage, and all would have been happy to reach the same place in half the time by a faster train. Not so in India. The people of the party, when informed of the change, staged a protest that threatened to disturb the joyful proceedings of an Indian wedding in the countryside. We have been cheated, they shouted. We have paid to be eight hours in the train and stop at every station, and now they want to send us away after four hours without stopping anywhere. The cheek of it! They think we can be taken in so easily? We want our money's worth and our full time in the train. And if they cannot do that, let them return half our money. We have not paid the full price to be kept only half the time in the train!

That was another kind of logic. For the wedding party the leisurely journey in congenial company was part of the celebrations spread out along several days of family rejoicing. Everything had been planned, discussed endless times, enjoyed in advance. And now these senseless railway officials wanted to disturb the first item of the festivities with their insensitive interference. A quick journey. An express train. Blind efficiency, when what is required is a slow pace in a comfortable atmosphere. These people had the ability to enjoy each event on its own without conditioning it to the next one; the wisdom to enjoy the journey instead of spoiling it with the haste to arrive. Everybody on the railway platform sided with the wedding party. Only I, lonely Westerner in an always surprising East, was left to wonder on the different attitudes to life that are held by different mentalities, and on the practical effects of those different attitudes. Peace of mind and friendliness with life seem to flower more easily in Eastern regions. Life runs to a different timetable. An Eastern wedding party is essentially different from a Western wedding party. And life is a wedding.

14

The Path Is the Goal

This is a hard saying by an Indian sage, Swami Ramdas: "The path is the goal; to walk is to reach." I call it hard because whenever I have quoted it before Western audiences I have noticed many faces clouded and eyebrows twisted in genuine puzzlement as to what exactly the saying means. The path is certainly different from the goal; it is the intermediary stage that is meant to lead to a distant and future goal, as the road to a city leads to the city, or long studies to the acquisition of knowledge. The road is not the city, and training for battle is not yet victory. Similarly, walking is entirely different from reaching. While walking we move, and in reaching we rest. Motion and rest are not the same, any more than wishing and obtaining. True, the Orient thrives on paradoxes, but we would like to know what is gained by identifying the effort to obtain with the result of achieving. Why does Ramdas say that the path is the goal?

If I am not too optimistic, the last chapter has prepared the way for this puzzle, and the answer may now come readily to the mind. The elevator and the train. Is the elevator "path" or "goal"? We know it now. For the executive it is a path, and for the children a goal. And Ramdas has taken the children's view, which fitted exactly with his own childlike and playful manner. The path we tread, at each step in our pilgrimage and each breath in our life, is of itself—for that fleeting moment but truly and deeply—the end and goal of our activity, fulfillment of our aims and plenitude of our being. Walking is reaching because each step reaches a point in our career which is the only one it can reach and was ever meant to reach. Walking is reaching . . . for the time being, but then that "time being" is the only time that exists at the moment, and so the action is total and complete in its instantaneous existence. Each day is valid in itself without waiting for the crowning of death and glory, and in the same way each instant is full and self-sufficient without the need of a final recognition to justify the present effort. We reach the final destination only by reaching day by day the partial aims of our limited scope. The more we are conscious of and grateful for the daily reaching, the happier our daily life will be.

This is no hair-splitting or abstract philosophy. Indeed, this is the most practical way to obtain a degree of peace and satisfaction now while right in the midst of all our work and all our doubts. I learn to find satisfaction in what I am doing; to realize that it is worthwhile, that each moment of my life is valid in itself, recorded forever in the annals of eternity on its own merit, whatever may follow after it on that day or in my whole life. Not to think of the total course, which is not in my hands right now, but of the present moment which I can enjoy in its ready fruition, all the more available because it is so small. By learning to live small instants, I shall realize someday that I have lived the big burden of a whole lifetime. We can fragment with profit the responsibility of a whole lifetime in order to lighten the task of serious living.

Not that there is no final goal, but that I am living it out in the concrete minute goals of daily living. Each of them, in the pretty accessibility of its smallness, is not precisely a part of an ultimate definitive goal to be achieved at the end, but is perfect in itself—as every meal is enjoyable without reference to the next one, and every morsel delectable without waiting for another bite. We have to redeem the validity of each instant if we want to capture the fullness of the whole. Think of a diamond: Each side is beautiful and each color different, and it is by emphasizing one by one the individuality of each facet that we realize the value of the whole.

To walk is to reach. I once tried the following stunt on an innocent friend. I was walking along the streets of the city when this friend saw me, stopped, and asked the usual starter: "Where are you going?" I was walking with Ramdas on my mind, and my answer was unusual. "Nowhere," I said. He looked puzzled for a moment, and then with a gesture of approval he nodded, understanding: "I see; you are going for your constitutional." "No," I said, "I am just going." His smile of understanding froze on his lips, and a shadow of worry crossed his forehead as a ripple caused by the unspoken thought that all was not well with me. I smiled my reassurance. "You see," I tried, "a moment ago I was walking, just as this moment I am standing and talking to you. I was not walking in order to meet you, and yet it so happened that I met you, and I welcome the meeting. I don't suppose you will ask me why I am talking to you; I am doing it because we are standing in front of each other and we are friends. In the same way I see no point in being asked why I am walking. Circumstances have combined to place me at this juncture in this public street, and I keep moving as the obvious thing to do without a further thought to it." By now my friend was lost, but I continued my lecture. "Yes, of course, I do remind myself now that there is a job I have to do and a place I have to reach and that I am on my way there. Yes, sure, that is true, and I could have given you that for an answer. But, if you don't mind my saying so, such an answer would have been as formal and empty as your question. You gain nothing by my telling you that I am going to the drugstore to buy a toothbrush. It is much more truthful and real and actual to tell you simply that I am going, that I am moving, just as I am now standing and talking and enjoying it. One thing at a time. When I stop talking with you and you move along, I know that my feet will keep going and will take me where they know they have to go. I am not going to be standing alone like a fool in the middle of the street. But at present yes, I am standing and that is all there is to it. Time to move along?"

I realized by that little encounter how hard it is for us, bred in a culture of tomorrows, to recover the sense of the present. All our life is, Where are you going? What are you planning? What are you expecting? What are you striving for? I myself found it funny and felt silly when I talked in that way to my friend. I was imposing on him my own philosophies, and trying out on him my own experiment in living. No wonder he left me with a polite greeting and a confused look. But I like to think aloud and to express before trusted friends these new ways of looking at the art of living. It is helpful to translate into language and dialogue the perspectives of a new understanding, however cumbersome our first efforts may be. The task is to rescue the present from the grip of the future.

A young man of great promise was in the midst of his Ph.D. studies when the doctors diagnosed terminal cancer with one or at the most two years more to live. That man wrote a beautiful letter to me in which he described his situation and analyzed candidly his own reaction to the news. His first impulse, after taking in the finality of the diagnosis, was to leave his studies, which in any case he would not now be able to complete, and dedicate whatever active time was left to him to some useful work in the service of others. He had recently been ordained a priest, but had not yet had much chance to exercise his priestly ministry, busy as he was with his studies. So that first impulse, as well as the advice of others, was that he should work directly helping people in their spiritual needs for as long as he would have the strength to do it. That would give him the satisfaction of working as a priest and knowing he would die having done good for others. Yet, on second and deeper thought, he changed his mind and decided to continue with his research and his thesis, knowing fully well that he would not live to complete it. The reason, as he explained it with the sharpness of his understanding and the sincerity that had always been his and was now heightened by the proximity of death, was illuminating. He said that his studies were a valid activity in themselves, and to leave them now half-way done for a last-hour hurried ministry would amount to saying that he had wasted his time, and that the only way to make up for a lost life was to have somehow a little priestly activity at the end of it. This he, wisely and deeply, refused to accept. His life was as precious and valid when studying for a thesis he would never write as when administering the sacraments or instructing the people of God. Otherwise, a student for the priesthood who died before being ordained would have to consider his life a waste, which it definitely is not. Each stage is fine by itself. Each hour of study is precious in itself, in the sincerity of the effort, the concentration of the mind, the discipline of the senses, the understanding of new facts, and the fulfillment of duty. We are so much examination-oriented that we consider a course wasted if the corresponding degree is not obtained. My friend was wiser. He had seen, with the light that was already coming to him from the other side of the horizon, that his preparation for an academic result and for the consequent educational activities was as true and worthy and legitimate as any future work in teaching and preaching could have been. No future successes are needed to justify today's efforts, just as no degree is needed to justify today's studies. A soldier's training is honorable even if he never goes to battle. He does not have to shoot anybody in order to prove that his training has been useful. All that we do is fine at the time we do it, independent of the results it may produce in the future. In our terminology, the path is the goal, and the study for a Ph.D. is as sacred and noble as the degree that may never be achieved. My friend died as the doctors had foreseen. He did not complete his Ph.D. thesis, but he completed a beautiful life and is still remembered with affection and admiration by all who knew him.

The path is the goal. Let us enjoy the path.

15

The Purpose
of Having No Purpose

Now a harder saying. Lao Tzu, the Chinese sage, sums up the wisdom of his teachings and the experience of his life in a disconcerting sentence that for a moment seems calculated to shock more than to illuminate. This is his summary autobiography: "Forever tarrying in purposelessness." Quite a program of life! The laziness to tarry, and the irresponsibility of having no purpose. And that forever. No purpose in any action and no purpose in life. And he seems to boast of it as he proclaims happily to the four winds the secret of his life and the core of his philosophy: Have no purpose, wait quietly, and be ready to keep that attitude forever. That is the gate of wisdom and the way to happiness. Try it for yourself, and you will soon realize that it is not so easy as it looks. Certainly not for a person who has been trained to fix objectives and to measure efforts. The point is, what exactly does he mean by that and how does it help? Unless we understand the doctrine we cannot be expected to feel very enthusiastic about it.

Here, again, what was said in the last chapter has, hopefully, prepared the way for the understanding of this one. In saying that the path is the goal, Ramdas was actually exhorting us to set aside all those remote goals that rule our lives at a distance, and to concentrate only on the present moment, on this single step. This means, in fact, forgetting the final goal, and Ramdas' goal is now Lao Tzu's purpose. The purpose, however noble and useful and necessary, is a thing of the future, and it is the future that we are learning to keep in check in order to give a chance to the present. That future purpose is fine if it helps to actualize and vivify the present; but if, as so often happens, the future goal becomes a crippling obsession, an impossible target, an enervating dream, then it is better kept in its place, which is farther down the calendar, and told to keep quiet till its day arrives. Lao Tzu's message is to drop the purpose and face the facts. Forget the dream and tackle reality. Lack of purpose does not mean lack of responsibility. On the contrary, it may very well mean an emphasis on responsibility to make us face the present situation in full earnest instead of escaping into long-range plans and faraway dreams.

I even suspect this to be the reason that we place so much stress on plans, objectives, ideals: We subconsciously want to escape the heavy burden of today's life by planning wholeheartedly for tomorrow's; we plot to avoid the present by filling our minds with the future, and to avoid action by drawing up plans of action; we shun realities by building up purposes. *We miss life by thinking about life.*

Another reason for our eagerness is that we transfer to our private life the methods that work for us in our public concerns. The running of an institution requires careful planning and constant feedback, and we sometimes apply to our inner life the method that works in our factories. But man is not a machine, and neither is the individual the same as the group. Let us not mix the procedures.

I am taking part in a staff meeting of a large educational institution. The theme of the meeting is: management by objectives. Each department has to fix in practical detail the objectives it can and means to achieve by the end of the year, and consequently at the end and the middle of each semester, and to set up a machinery to periodically review the situation and assess the progress. Results can be quantified, and at the end of the year we shall know with almost uncomfortable precision how each department has performed. It is a hard procedure that is going to keep everybody on his or her toes for the year, but it is healthy and necessary if we want to run an institution with efficiency and responsibility. I sit through all that and approve all that. The trouble begins for me when I attempt, as I have done numberless times in my life, to run my life also as a staff meeting, and to apply to my life management by objectives. The goals to be achieved in my spiritual, intellectual, and social life, the means to be used to achieve them, and a fixed timetable to mark the time limit for each concrete goal—all very neatly typed out and kept in view for daily check. A praiseworthy effort. And a useless enterprise. My private office does not work better and production does not improve. The future has smothered the present. The planning has dampened the thrill. The objectives, instead of being stepping stones to success, have become stumbling stones to frustration. By projecting myself onto future horizons I have lost contact with the present ones, and loss of contact with reality is the greatest loss in life.

"Probably there was never such a purposeful, scheming civilization as our own, a people that lived so entirely for the future and with so great a degree of anxiety for the morrow. There was never, for that reason, such a meaningless civilization."* These words from Alan Watts are apt to make us think. We are a people "that lives entirely for the future," full of plans, aims, ideals, objectives, goals, and perspectives. There has never been such a "futurization" of human life as there is now. Financially we save for the future, subscribe to a provident fund, insure our lives and sign up for a retirement plan before we can even afford

* Alan Watts, *Behold the Spirit*, Vintage Books, 1972, p. 179.

it. This financial behavior is only a material reflection of our emotional behavior. Emotionally also we live in the future, and that explains the tension in which modern man lives: "so great a degree of anxiety for the morrow." A psychologist defines anxiety as "the gap between the now and the then"—that is, the distance between the present and the future—and so a people that lives in the future is condemned, as we are, to live in the dark gap of anxiety. Anxiety is the burden of the future on the weakness of the present. The more purposeful we are, the more anxious we become. Our lives know of that unhappy equation.

Yet the most striking conclusion Alan Watts draws from his diagnosis is the last one: "There was never, for that reason, such a meaningless civilization." This is an apparent paradox that hides a brilliant truth. At first sight it would seem that life, or, for that matter, any individual action, draws its meaning from its purpose; therefore the greater the purpose, the clearer the meaning. In fact it happens the other way around: Purpose and meaning are in inverse ratio; the more of the one, the less of the other. The reason is evident, and has a full bearing on what we are trying to understand here: Purpose refers to the future, and meaning to the present, and so the more of the future, the less of the present. We have burdened life and its stages and activities with so many and worthy purposes that its meaning has been buried under them. Everything I do or plan to do on this busy earth is so fraught with purposes ahead in this life and in the next that I literally cannot see the forest for the trees. I cannot see the present, busy as I am with understanding the manifold results of my actions upon the future; and so I have a lot of purpose that will be achieved later, and no meaning to be enjoyed now. Much good will be accomplished in some more or less remote future by the sundry activities that fill my days now, and I will be happy to see and to rejoice at that good when it comes to pass. But for the time being I would like to have something I can grasp and can hold as of now, something to steady my feet and fill my heart as they are with me now, not in a future realm beyond my reach for days to come. Briefly and pointedly: We live "in order to," and it is time we learn just to "live." Drop purposes and start living. "Forever tarrying in purposelessness" was the motto of a man who enjoyed every minute of his life with every cell of his being. *Purposelessness* is a bad word with us. We might get new insights into ways of making the best of our earthly condition if we came to terms with that unshapely word.

Why did Mozart write music? To pay his bills, to be sure, and to humor the moods of Archbishop Colloredo; but this answer, however true and practical, only hides the truer and deeper one. Mozart wrote music because he was bursting with it inside himself, because he enjoyed himself immensely while doing it, because it was his very nature, his temper, his genius. To say that Mozart's purpose in writing music was to earn money is perfectly true and perfectly useless. Mozart's music, in the real and genuine sense of it, had no purpose, and precisely in that lies its lasting freshness and its immortal beauty. A purpose commercializes music . . . as it commercializes life. A true artist knows how to revel in purposelessness.

Children are artists. And children have no purpose in their unceasing multifarious activity. Why do you throw a ball, why do you dig a hole, why do you run, why do you dance? Why? Ask the question and miss the fun. Children play because they enjoy playing; and it will be beautiful when we can say that we live because we enjoy living. No more philosophies will be needed when we become like little children. Then we shall discover the Kingdom of God, which is already within us.

An eager youth went to a Japanese master to learn the martial arts. He asked, "How long will it take me?" The master answered, "Five years."—"That is a long time. If I work twice as hard as your other students, how long will it take me?"—"Ten years."—"And if I redouble my efforts and work day and night?" —"Then it will take twenty years."—"Sir, how is it that every

time I double my effort you double the time?"—"Because if you
fix one eye on the goal, you have only one eye left to find the
way."

"How many tennis games have been lost by thinking about
winning while returning a serve?" asks Stewart Holmes in *Zen
Art for Meditation*. And Michael Gelb in *Body Learning* seems to
answer the question with his own experience: "Once I had to
play a game of tennis against a tough adversary. I had already
lost the first set, and was trailing behind in the second by two
games to four. Till that moment I had made a desperate effort
not to be eliminated, and my forehead was dripping with perspiration. Suddenly I was struck by the thought of my helpless
situation and its importance for mankind's future evolution, and
the whole humor of the moment dawned upon me. In an instant, my attention shifted from the future (Who will win? What
will I say if I lose?) to the present (the touch of the racket, the
smell of earth from the ground). Without thinking of it I began
to play superbly. I won the second set, and the third was drawn
at six games, which forced a follow-up. I remember with perfect
clarity my feeling of detachment at that time, in spite of the
presence of my coach and the spectators around us. During the
follow-up I played the best tennis of my life, winning each point
without effort. *Something* won the game. In those 'peak' or 'creative' moments I find that the distinction between ends and
means vanishes, and leaves me with the realization of the Eternal
Present."†

†Michael Gelb, *Body Learning*, Aurum Press Limited, p. 90.

16

When to Climb a Summit

The idea is important, and I want to clarify it and deepen it. A purpose in life and action helps to summon strength, focus energies, and bring out the best in a person's ability to achieve a concrete aim in an appointed time. On the other hand, a purpose also distracts from the present, projects the mind into the future, cuts off contact, and blurs reality. I will describe here a very simple experience to illustrate both points.

I love to roam along the mountain paths of Mount Abu in Rajasthan where I have spent many a happy holiday among wild rocks and thick jungle, with the occasional sight of a bear or a panther at recklessly short distance. The highest peak is Gurushikhar, whose climb is no mountaineering feat but a steady and at times breathless two-hour path up from the village. I start in the early morning, alone with nature, keeping the summit in sight with the resolve to reach it and win the priceless reward of a limitless horizon till the plains of India become sky in the distance, and the landscape of Pakistan is guessed under the faraway mist in the brotherly continuity of a geographical embrace. I get tired after some time, the sun gains height and intensity, my breathing gets shorter and shorter, and a moment comes when I begin to think it will be wise to abandon the climb, turn back, and reach home quietly in time for lunch. What need do I have for new records, who is asking me to get there, what do I gain by seeing once more what I have seen so many times? Nobody knows I have come, and in any case I need not prove myself to anybody and least of all to myself. Let me call it a day and go back from here.

Such are my thoughts in the fatigue and perspiration of the long climb. But then the summit is there. I have determined I am going to reach it today. I can see it with increasing sharpness as I draw near: the conical temple, the large bell outside, the niche that protects the stone footprints of guru Dattatreya. I have set myself a goal and I mean to reach it. An aimless walk could have gone on more or less at my will, but today the summit beckons to me, casts a spell on me, gives strength to my feet and rhythm to my lungs, and keeps me going till I reach the goal and stand on the top and fill my chest with winds from the four cardinal points and regale my sight with the boundless view. I have done it. If the summit had not been there, I would not have found the strength to make the effort and would have given up half-way. But the concrete aim makes me forget fatigue and ignore heat. I reach because there *is* somewhere to reach and I am determined to reach there. My walk is longer because I have a goal.

But then another day I start in the same way, only that my thoughts change as I walk along. I had again meant to climb Gurushikhar today, but at a point along the way I realize I am so intent on reaching that I am not enjoying the walking. It is not only the view from the top that is unique and rewarding, but the view from each point on the way, and the way itself—the slopes and the trees, the ravines and the creeks, the changing shades of green, the wild fowl running on the dry leaves, and the vultures drawing circles in the sky. I am missing my walk by coveting the summit. Let it go for today. I will slow my step and forget the distance. I will turn back at any moment I want and will not overstress myself to reach any preconceived goal. The walk is perfect and complete in itself wherever I turn, summit or no summit. Let my feet find their way and my body tell me when it wants to go back. There is leisure in my body and peace in my soul. No Gurushikhar today. No temple bell and no sacred footprints. And yet, a glorious morning.

This illustrates a clear difference in the ways one can proceed on the walk that is life. A purpose helps to climb summits. A no-purpose helps to enjoy the landscape. Both things are good, and both have their times. To be always climbing summits takes away the joy of life. To walk always aimlessly leads nowhere. The wisdom to combine both attitudes is part of the difficult art of life.

In my understanding, the effort to climb summits, the setting up of ideals, the pursuit of high goals in life, the desire to change the world and reform society fits in better with our youthful years; these things then fire us with zeal, get us moving and make us strain every nerve to improve ourselves and do good to others. If we have no summit in view and no ideal in mind we are not likely to be shaken out of our natural laziness, to outreach ourselves and give of our best. We need motivation, dreams, incentives to set out energetically upon the arduous task of living. And we usually do begin that way. Our first years in training and in work are happily marked by high idealism, set purpose, and unremitting effort. That is a glorious beginning. Let there be many Gurushikhars in our life, many Himalayas, and many Everests. All will be needed to bring to flower the many potentialities hidden under layers of diffidence and shyness and fear. It takes a purposeful effort to get us started in life and work amidst opposition and indifference. Without a vigorous push we would never get going. All that is fine and necessary and welcome. If there were no summits we would never climb.

The danger comes when we try to spend all our lives climbing summits. We have acquired such a habit of climbing, of reaching out, of setting up goals, of conceiving purposes, of aiming high and conquering summits that we are not at peace unless we are engaged in some noble enterprise or other. And then comes the most delicate stage of our life, hard at times to see because it is humiliating and painful to acknowledge it. The fact is that purposes are not achieved, dreams do not come true, summits are not climbed. The world remains pretty much the same as it was when we came on the stage, and we ourselves drag along our weaknesses and idiosyncrasies much as we knew them when we started out and swore to set ourselves right and the world with us. The result is frustration. The effort has been great, and the result modest. The bow has been permanently tense, and it now seems impossible to bend it more, and ignominious to put it down. We cannot climb any more, and we cannot do without climbing. We would lose our self-respect if we gave up climbing. And yet we see now that we are doing it to no purpose. Too many goals and too many failures. Here a permanent disappointment may set in, a veiled cynicism, a hardened formalism, with the burdensome task of carrying on as before without our earlier feelings of zest and zeal.

This is the moment when the word "purposelessness" can begin to make sense in a positive way, with summits removed, goals cut down to size, dreams known for what they are, and the leisurely walk of life resumed without a set map, timing, or destination. It takes a bit of humor to do that, a good deal of practical humility, and an advanced maturity. The work we perform will still have an external goal, an official motivation, a measurable result; but we shall go about it with a light heart and an easy mind, not burdened by the need to achieve or the anxiety to succeed. We can deceive the world by taking with outward seriousness what we inwardly know to be a game and a play. We shall give the right answers to the right questions, while in our hearts we do not give undue importance to what is not intrinsically important. Freedom from the need to reach, to show, to perform is a great condition for lasting peace of mind. And the gentle loosening of our grip on big and small purposes for life and work is a vital step in the attaining of that freedom. There is wisdom in the paradoxical advice of purposelessness.

Woody Allen, as Zelig in the 1983 movie of the same name, faces a nervous breakdown as he finds himself without a purpose to live for, without meaning in life to give strength and direction to whatever he can do or be. A friend advises him to go and see a rabbi who will explain to him the meaning of life and the purpose of our existence in this world, so that he will be reassured and helped through his crisis. He goes, and a few days later he meets his friend again. As he still looks definitely downcast, his friend asks him, "Did you meet the rabbi?"—"Yes," he answers rather miserably.—"And did he explain to you the meaning of life?"—"Oh, yes, he did, rather thoroughly . . ."—"But . . ."—"But he spoke in Hebrew!" That was a wise rabbi indeed. Maybe Lao Tzu is after all closer than we think to the Talmud.

17

India's Secret

The Indian languages have a word, taken from Sanskrit, that sums up pointedly the Indian approach to action in life—and, even more, the whole Oriental mentality and the open secret of the peace of mind it inspires and fosters in the midst of our troubled civilization. The word is *"karma-phal-tyag."* *Karma* means action, *phal* is fruit or result, and *tyag* is a gentle giving up, dropping, being detached from. Thus the word means "action-fruit-detachment," or "detachment from the results of our actions." The Gita expresses through this its whole philosophy of activity without anxiety; and Gandhi based on it the whole movement for Indian independence, and achieved the greatest historical feat of our age, the freedom of India, while keeping his peace of mind and trying to teach the same attitude to his countrymen and to the world at large—a lesson which we have still to learn.

Full activity in whatever we are doing, full action, full involvement; and at the same time genuine inner detachment from the result that may come from our efforts. No pride if we succeed, and no despondency if we fail. We do our duty in carrying out whatever is expected of us, and then we leave the result in the hands of God with noble indifference and inner peace. Human action is beneficent only when man is detached from the fruit of his action. Only then can he keep his soul at rest while engaged in wholehearted activity.

Western mentality is essentially result-oriented. A prize is put on efficiency, productivity, achievement. What counts is the final result, and no effort, however well meant and well done, is good enough if at the end it is the competitor that bags the profitable contract or the rival candidate that gets the job. In business it is the final figure that matters, the net profit, the upward graph. To show results, to deliver the goods—that is the only method to make a way for oneself in our competitive society, to carve a career, to reach the top. To study is not enough if one does not get the degree, to advertise is not enough if one does not sell the product. Everybody demands results, and so everybody wants results and cannot move ahead without them. Even in our spiritual endeavors we were exhorted to "draw fruit" from our daily meditation, and in the Spiritual Exercises of St. Ignatius the retreatant is not allowed to pass on to the "Second Week" until he has obtained the "fruit" of the First. This is a perfectly legitimate attitude in a context of purposes and objectives . . . and perfectly unintelligible to an Oriental for whom contemplation is enough reward in itself without looking for any subsequent fruit deriving from it. The fact is that results count in the West in almost any field and for almost everybody. And to that emphasis the West owes its purposefulness, its industriousness, and its efficiency.

The trouble with being result-oriented is that the result is essentially a thing of the future, and so a tension is established between the effort made today and the fruit to be harvested tomorrow. If I am studying now, but my purpose is to pass the examination next month, that situation establishes a gap between the present and the future, which is anxiety; this makes me feel tense and nervous till the examination comes and the result is announced. Emphasis on the result keeps me waiting till it comes, only to begin a new period of waiting for the next result from the next effort. But if, on the contrary, my mind is trained to concentrate on the work at hand and to be detached from the future result whatever it may be and whenever it may come, I can find peace in my work and avoid the tension of waiting for its consequences. This is difficult to do in an examination, but in climates and atmospheres where this attitude is lived, it comes about naturally and eases the burden of living.

I shall never forget the charming spontaneity with which the present publisher of my Gujarati works introduced himself to me at our first business meeting years ago. "I am a non-matric," he said with candid admission. I knew the expression and treasured the moment. "Matric" is short for the matriculation examination that qualifies the Indian student for entrance into the university; and "non-matric" describes the individual who has appeared for the examination and has failed in it, thereby terminating his academic career at the doors of the university. Now, that expression embodies a whole conception and way of life which is the one I am trying to describe here. The man could say with perfect self-respect, "I am a non-matric," just as someone else would say, "I am a Ph.D." His duty was not to pass the examination but to prepare for it and take it. He has taken his examination, and that is the end of his worries. He has done his "work" and prescinds from its "fruit." To pass him or not to pass him is now the responsibility of the examiners, and they will do their duty and announce the result. He has not passed. Fine. He is a non-matric. He was detached from the fruit of his action (the Gita is lived in India in its practical mentality even by people who have never read it), and goes on cheerfully to whatever work life may offer him next. No traumas and no regrets. The man states his qualification and we go on to business. How I wish I could say with the same ease that I am a non-saint, a non-mystic, a non-contemplative! That I have tried my best, I have taken the examination, and I have received no degree in the courses of the spirit. That I am a non-matric. Great. I keep up my work under God's loving gaze, and I know that he has as much use for those who do not make the grade as for those who have. My non-matric publisher is doing a good job with my books.

Rudyard Kipling in *Kim* gives an earlier example of the same idiom, which may not be appreciated by the noninitiated reader. When Kim's friend, the Lama, dictates a letter to Father Victor about him, the official letter-writer identifies himself in the document as follows: "Written by Sobrao Satai, Failed Entrance Allahabad University." That was his proud status. He had taken the entrance examination to Allahabad University and had failed in it. A reliable letter-writer.

Unfortunately Western thought and values are making inroads into the East, and all the evil aspects of the examination system that we inherited with colonialism are also felt here. Examination results do generate anxiety among students and their parents, and the teaching of the Gita begins to get clouded by competition, anxiety, malpractices in the mad rush to obtain a degree and land a job. The achieving society is extending its grip to the plains of the Ganges. Many conquerors have come to India only to be conquered themselves in the end. If India eventually wins and keeps its traditional identity under the new wave, that will be its greatest service to modern society.

To me this is the deepest and most radical difference between East and West, and the understanding of this difference can help people on both sides of the globe (which, of course, has no sides). I have written about this somewhere else, and I indulge in the luxury of quoting myself. "In the West everything has a purpose. Man is created to praise, adore and serve God our Lord, the student studies to pass the examination, the worker works to earn a salary, marriage is for children, and food is for life. Every action must have its 'final cause,' which directs, determines, motivates human behavior and defines each person in the ways of life, as the final cause is, in scholastic parlance, the first to be conceived and the last to be achieved. But such a purpose, with the effort, expectation and evaluation that it unavoidably brings with itself, conditions, limits, narrows the horizon of life at the moment of existence. The purpose sacrifices the present to the future. That is why the Orient disowns all purpose. Everything is what it is, every event is valid in itself, every instant is eternity. We need not look for the value of the present moment in the future fruit it may bring forth. No. Today's action is what it is in existential plenitude, without any need of future happy consequences to justify itself. Freedom from purpose is a condition of peace, of mental balance, of moment-to-moment satisfaction in an ever changing world. To live in the present is eternal wisdom, and the price to be paid is the surrender of purposes and goals. Detachment from the fruits of one's action is the way to action with peace" (*Razón y Fe*, August 1988).

I say that there is a price to be paid. The price is clear, and, to Western eyes, heavy. The price is the devaluation of efficiency and excellence as aims of our earthly endeavor. If the result does not matter, then the urge to do well, the ideal of efficiency, and the glamour of excellence lose their appeal, and the quality of the work is bound to suffer. It does. The West is noted for efficiency, the East is not, marking the difference between working for results and feeling indifferent to them. The Indian worker is concerned with being at his place from eleven in the morning till five in the afternoon, and performing quietly whatever operations he has to perform without a special hurry or a compelling target. He is there, and he does what he has been told to do. Whether or not the machine he manufactures will work—that is not his concern; he is detached from the fruit of his action. However, the buyer of the machine may not be, and may even have the effrontery to complain if the machine does not work properly. The worker has done his job, has kept to his time schedule, and thereby has fulfilled his duty. Such an attitude may help the worker keep his peace of mind while he works, but it certainly does not make for efficiency. David McClelland in his book *Power: The Inner Experience* gives several examples of this attitude in India. I will relate here some examples of my own experience.

I have mentioned the mountains of Abu and my friendship with them. In the midst of them there is a beautiful lake, carved by the gods with their nails, and on the shore of that lake the enterprising Abu municipality decided to build a public garden. An ornament in that garden was to be an umbrella-shaped shelter under which several people could sit to contemplate the waters and the boats and the large fish that own the lake under a strictly observed no-fishing notice. The umbrella was duly put up; I watched the workers set up the wooden casing, pour the cement, and wait for it to set so that the outward casing could be removed and the umbrella stand in all its splendor. The appointed day came, and I witnessed the careful proceedings. The planks of wood were removed carefully, the last support being taken away simultaneously by several workers all around who stood back at once to admire the finished work. What they admired, and I with them, was the prompt and sudden collapse of the whole structure. The whole umbrella descended gently onto the ground, and the pieces of broken cement formed an irregular circle where their shadow was meant to have been. Nobody was hurt, and indeed I got the suspicion that they had been expecting the result after experiencing previous such collapses in other works.

What brought me back to reality was their reaction. When their work collapsed, they all simultaneously burst into a loud laughter. Great! I would have expected an expression of concern, grief, disappointment, mutual recrimination, and fear of an inquiry and the ensuing unpleasantness for all concerned. Nothing of the kind. They just enjoyed the fun, collected the broken pieces, and cleared out. They had done their job, and there was no more to it. Their job had been to prepare the mold and pour the cement. Whether the structure then stood or fell was not their concern. And nobody else cared. There was no inquiry, no unpleasantness . . . and no umbrella. That was a concerted action and a nonexisting fruit. I wonder if that was the attitude contemplated by the Gita, but it was at any rate its practical application. The good mood of the workers was safeguarded at the cost of efficiency.

At a little distance from the lake there is a small bridge over a river that feeds the lake. The bridge was rebuilt, and now it mercifully withstood the weight of the traffic. But not without a hitch. On both sides of the bridge long horizontal iron bars had been fixed as a handrail to prevent pedestrians from falling into the river. The new bridge was solemnly inaugurated in the morning, and that first night all the iron handrail bars were stolen by someone who undoubtedly proposed to put them to a better use. The next morning the bridge appeared without the protective rails. They were never replaced. Here again the municipality had done its duty by providing the fixture that went with the bridge. The permanent result of a reasonable protection for passing pedestrians was not the issue. The implied message was that you do your duty and ignore the result. Pedestrians have to be careful now when crossing the bridge. And no one complains.

George Mikes had a similar experience in Japan. "The air-conditioning in our hotel room went wrong every day, so that the room was either unbearably hot or was suddenly turned into a refrigerator, nay a deep freeze. Every day we asked the clerk at the front desk to have it repaired. Every other day our request was noted with exquisite courtesy, then ignored. But every other-other day a little man appeared with portable steps and a torch. He came in, bowed deeply and smiled. Then he ascended the steps, switched on his torch and flashed it around the grille. He came down, smiled, picked up his steps and departed. Next day I would go to the front desk, smile, bow and complain again, telling them that we were melting or freezing. This complaint stigmatized me as a boorish and hopelessly ill-mannered *gaijin* (foreigner). Had not the man *been?* It was quite immaterial— from the point of view of a higher, oriental philosophy— whether he had mended the air-conditioning or not. His appearance clearly proved that my first complaint had been accepted, looked into, treated with respect—so what more did I want?"*

It is interesting that this experience comes from Japan, and the victim attributes it to a "higher, oriental philosophy." Traditional Japan shares with India, through Buddhism, the cult of the present, and, consequently, the veiling of the future and its results with intended indifference. Modern Japan, on the other hand, worships efficiency and demands results. The tension between the two opposite approaches is having an affect on the modern Japanese generation. The dilemma is whether peace of mind should prevail at the expense of efficiency, or efficiency with the heavy price of anxiety. The ideal, of course, would be to combine the good elements in each of these attitudes and achieve practical efficiency while keeping one's peace of mind. In the genial expression of the Japanese manual for motorcycle repairing, "the first condition to repair a motorcycle is to have peace of mind." This, however, is not easy, especially for those of us who have emphasized throughout our lives the importance of results, success, perfectionism, and achievement of concrete goals within a prescribed time; it is difficult for us to undertake a task with full commitment and the interest in doing it well, a job with a measurable result under quality control—and to keep all the while an unruffled mind come what may.

Gurdjieff taught his disciples this lesson in a rather drastic way. He would order them to build a house in full detail, only to oblige them to pull it down as soon as they had finished it. A rather radical approach, much in his own style, to get them used

* G. Mikes, *The Land of the Rising Yen*, Penguin Books, 1985, p. 77.

to working with full zest without paying attention to results. A rather striking version of the detachment from the fruit of one's actions.

The Gita has another interesting word: *nishkam-karma*; this means "work-without-attachment," and Gandhi was called *karma-yogi* or "the yogi in action," the man who practices the discipline, detachment, concentration, contemplation of Yoga in the midst of a committed activity, even the herculean task of freeing a great country from a mighty empire. Across the centuries I find a familiar echo in the example of my spiritual father St. Ignatius who was defined by Nadal as a "contemplative in action." Maybe we have neglected the contemplation while plunging into the action. It is time for us to regain the balance.

18

The Dancing Feet

Two Zen masters had their favorite disciples who, not being yet fully enlightened, rivaled each other in mutual encounters and sought to defeat each other in discussion. They met daily on their way to the village and prepared their questions to outwit each other with unexpected repartee. One day the first disciple asked the second as they met along the way: "Where are you going?" The second answered: "I am going where my feet are going." The first was chastened by the surprising answer and remained silent for the rest of the way. Back home he told his master about his discomfiture, and the master advised him: "Tomorrow ask him the same question, and when he says, 'I am going where my feet are going,' ask him, 'And if you had no feet, where would you be going?' That will settle him." So the disciple again asked his rival on the next day: "Where are you going?" He answered: "I am going where the wind is blowing." The first disciple again reported his defeat, and his master instructed him: "Tomorrow when he answers, 'I am going where the wind is blowing,' ask him, 'And if there was no wind, where would you be going?' and you will have him." The disciple tried his question again on the third day: "Where are you going?" And his walking companion answered nonchalantly: "I am going to the market to buy vegetables." With that the story ends.

That story delights me. The disciple goes where his feet are going. This seems at first thought an irresponsible answer, but among Zen students it is full of meaning. The feet know as the mind knows and the whole body knows. Man is all of a piece, and his organism is informed of his intentions as they well up within him. He is going to the market, and his feet are taking him there. What he will do when he reaches the market will also come up within him when the moment arrives and he finds himself in the marketplace. One thing at a time. Attention to the present moment. Trusting the body that is man's best friend. And the lighthearted sense to dance along the way at the rhythm of the feet that know their job and play their game. And it is not only the feet that are to be taken into confidence, but the whole of nature, and the path and the trees and the clouds and the wind. I am going where the wind is blowing. It too knows and directs and accompanies man's pilgrimage on earth and the disciple's way to the market. The wind, in Christian connotation, is the Spirit that blows where he wills, and we do not know where it comes from and where it goes but we trust the origin and follow the lead. The wind is not to be resisted and not to be ignored. The voice of nature, the wisdom of creation, the signs of the times. Move ahead cheerfully, play with the breeze and listen to its message.

And so the disciple can also say, truly and matter-of-factly, "I am going to the market to buy vegetables." It all comes to the same. His three expressions are only translations, at different levels, of the same simple fact. It can be expressed in the straightforward purpose of buying vegetables, in the cosmic consciousness of following the wind, or in the seemingly purposeless activity of letting one's feet find their way unhindered. It is the attitude that changes. Most of us spend our lives going to the market to buy vegetables. It is the rare soul, the enlightened master who can play the lovely game of following his feet.

That is, in fact, the answer to a famous *koan*, or Zen riddle: "Why did Bodhidharma go to China?" Bodhidharma was the

Buddhist monk who went from India to China in the sixth century and established Zen there. The answer, therefore, is historically plain and simple. One could ask in a parallel way, Why did Francis Xavier go to India? or, Why did Marco Polo go to China? or, Why did Columbus go to America? They all went for a definite purpose, whether to spread Christianity, to open new routes to commerce and adventure, or to discover new lands. Concrete purposes that motivated and made possible new feats in history. In the same way the textbook answer to the question, Why did Bodhidharma go to China? is simply that he went to spread Buddhism in those lands. But the koan is not so simple, and its answer never straightforward. The koan is meant to tease the mind out of ordinary thought, to defy logic, to surprise with the newness of a nonrational reason. The esoteric answer to the koan, "Why did Bodhidharma go to China?" is disarmingly, "Because his feet took him there."

Why am I writing this book? Because my fingers are hitting the keys on the typewriter. Fine answer. But if I give that answer to a friend or to a publisher, the best I can expect is an indulgent smile. Yes, there are purposes in their minds and in mine, but there is also something true and beautiful in the outrageous answer. There are thoughts in my mind and desires in my heart, there is life in my body and blood in my veins, and my fingers are itching with all that vitality that is within me and is a dream in my mind and love in my heart, movement in my limbs . . . and a wild urge to hit typewriter keys with the tips of my fingers. Let my fingers dance on the keyboard to the tune of the music in my mind, and let their steps trace the intricate filigree that marks the passing along of human thought through the medium of paper and ink. Let me forget my purposes, my contracts, my plans, my royalties, my readers, my critics, and write purely for the sake of writing without a care on my soul or a plan in my mind. Let my fingers do the job; they know me, they *are* me, and they have full right to play as they please and then put down to my account whatever they do. I stand by them, I accept their work and enjoy their dance. The dancing fingers; the dancing feet; symbol and instrument of the best work on earth because it is at the same time the best art.

Every reflective writer knows that the best book is the book that writes itself. No effort, no forced labor, no long night hours. Just the open sky and the friendly breeze, the sudden thought, the bold image, and the teasing word. They come on their own and hold their sway. The ideas flow as the feet dance. The words sprout as the birds fly. No worry and no overwork. Too much planning, researching, sketching, checking, polishing, rewriting may show scholarship and attain perfection, but will not recreate the soul with creativity and imagination. Let the book write itself —let the ideas find their way, and let the words fit by themselves into their places. They know with whom they want to go and by whose side they want to sit on the blank paper. It is their kingdom, their field, their playground. Let them use it as they please. It is their game. When they are allowed to play by themselves, the game flourishes and the earth rejoices. When the effort shows, the charm disappears. The happy day in the life of a writer is the day when he almost does not know what he is writing, when he is a medium, a channel, the agent of an overwhelming power that pulsates through him and dictates heavenly rhymes in newly born language. He wonders at what his hands write, and recognizes in obvious humility that he is hardly touching the waves that pass through him in sudden inspiration. The book writes itself while he watches with astonished eyes and a grateful heart. The feet walk by themselves and one has only to follow their direction. The dancing feet. The secret of joy.

There is more than meets the eye in the seemingly lightheaded aproach of following one's feet to wherever they are going. Aims and objectives may not be so essential to our progress as we have made them to seem. A little bit of aimless wandering may do us good. It is a legitimate way of exploring the jungle that is life. If nothing else, the foregoing considerations may have helped to make the word "purposelessness" appear somewhat respectable. Such, indeed, was my purpose.

19

The Beggar and the King

"I'll come to your house for Christmas. I'm sorry I cannot come now, it is totally impossible for me to find time these days, but at Christmas I'll surely have time, I'll remember and I'll make it a point to come and visit you."—"Do you promise?"—"I promise. I'll see you at your house during Christmas."

A simple promise I made in full good faith, meaning to fulfill it and rejoicing at having made it, as I liked the man and looked forward to visiting him in his home. There had been no undue insistence on his part and no compulsion on mine; only a genuine invitation and a grateful acceptance. A promise freely made and freely received in a spirit of friendship. Both felt happy about it at the moment. The assurance that I would visit him later made up to him for his disappointment about being unable to count on my visit now; and my pledge to come for Christmas soothed for me the unavoidable refusal to come now. As the present action was not possible I put in its place the promise of a future action. Common procedure—and common mistake. That simple and genuine promise got me into trouble, as promises usually do even when they are well meant and freely given. Why do promises cause trouble?

A promise causes trouble because it is a thing of the future, and the future is not in my hands and I do not know how it will turn out. When giving a promise I give something which is not mine to give, I give a date that has not yet arrived, and pledge an action that I do not know whether I shall be in a condition to perform. To give a promise is to borrow time, and borrowing can bring trouble.

That happened to me. Christmas arrived and I was as busy as ever and could not, however I tried, find an afternoon free to visit my friend. I remembered my promise and did my best, but I could not see any way to keep my word. Then I experienced clearly the double bind the promise had tied me into. If I decided to honor my promise, canceled important work and went somehow to my friend's house, I would do it at my inconvenience, and would resent my friend for it—without any fault of his, of course, but with anger against myself for having bound myself to do something which would seriously inconvenience me if I did it now. And if I did not go to visit him at Christmas as I had promised, there would be no end to his reproaches against me and my own reproaches against myself. "You promised, and you did not come." "I promised him and I did not keep my promise." Regrets both ways. Bad if I go, and bad if I don't. I am trapped in a trap of my own making. I gave what was not mine to give, and I cannot make good my gift. I suffer, and I have only myself to blame for it.

Can't I then make any promise? I could well have told my friend, "Listen, I have a genuine desire to come to your house; I cannot do it just now, but I imagine I shall be having time at Christmas, and if that is the case I will definitely come and see you; I'll let you know." That is fair enough and precludes all trouble. It shows my desire and admits my limitation. I want to come, and will do so if I get the time. But there is no promise and no bond. There will be no recriminations if the date arrives and the visit does not come through. And the visit will be all the more enjoyable if it does come through.

A beggar came to King Yuddhisthir in the Mahabharata when the king had just closed down the daily alms-giving session. The king told him, "Today's time is over; come tomorrow and I'll give you something." The beggar wanted assurance: "Will you surely give me alms if I come tomorrow?" The king, known for his munificence and his truthfulness, quieted him: "Of course I will give you; who has ever doubted the largess of the king?" Then the beggar ran through the whole city shouting at the top of his voice: "Come all, come all! Come and see the miracle! Let us celebrate the glory of our king! He has obtained victory over mortal time and has become a god. He knows what is going to happen tomorrow, he knows that he will be alive and he will give me alms! Great is our king and our god! Come to honor him!" The king heard the noise and asked its cause. When his servants reluctantly told him, he admitted: "The beggar has been king, and the king beggar. He has taught me a lesson today: I don't know whether I shall be able to give him anything tomorrow."

Every time we make a promise, we exceed our rights. We dispose of a future which is not ours. Yet we are radically reluctant to admit this and give up our supposed rights. Everybody has heard or read the eternal words, "I will love you forever," and every romance in every age and in all literary styles is based on those words. Yet those words are a clear if forgivable abuse on the part of whoever utters them. And in fact the literary plot often emerges when those eternal words lose their eternity and are now said by the same lover to a second beloved, to the distress of the first. A more positive and realistic expression of the same feeling would be: "I love you with all my heart, I want to love you always as I love you now, and I cannot imagine that I could ever cease to love you or that I could love you less. What the future will bring, however, in my feelings and in our relationship, I do not know. I give now what I can give, and I hope and pray I can continue to do the same throughout our lives." This is more exactly true, but I am afraid such a cautious declaration would not fit easily into poems and novels for ready effect. So the eternal words continue to be said, and the eternal quarrels continue to arise. Let us, then, make promises if we must, but let us understand their limitations, and not overstep into a future which is not ours. In fact, the better we understand and accept our limitations, the greater chance has our love to last and to weather the storms that will inevitably blow over it. "I love you now and want to love you always." That is a sensible lover.

A resolution is a promise of myself to myself, and so the same principle applies. I will stop smoking. I will never get angry again. I will get up every day at five in the morning. This attitude of self-improvement and planned self-reform can be very noble and show deep awareness of our shortcomings and genuine sincerity about overcoming them. As it involves the future, however, it also has to be treated with humility and caution. For all my desire and will power, I cannot guarantee what I shall do tomorrow when my alarm clock goes off dutifully at five in the morning, much less what I shall do a month or three months or a year from now. I just do not know. And if I have bound myself with a solemn promise to get up at five, and I am still between my bedsheets at seven, I am likely to indulge in a fit of self-recrimination, disappointment, and disgust which will be far worse than the understandable weakness of late rising. The beggar in the Mahabharata would undoubtedly have something to say about such behavior.

Promises and resolutions are fine if kept within bounds and understood for what they are. They are in themselves "declarations of intent" which show our present attitude and the attending desire that it should last and stand firm as the days pass and life goes on—with a prayer to God that he may bless our efforts and steady our steps along the daily path. Maybe Jesus' saying applies to this too, that our talk should be plain Yes and No, and anything beyond that is harmful. No pledges and no oaths, but the open inclination of the heart under grace, and the trust in faith that the future will take care of itself if we live our present to the full.

Yes, if I am able to come to your house at Christmas I'll feel very happy. I'll let you know whether I can make it when the time comes. Full affection and no binds. Our friendship is safe . . . for the time being, which is all we can say now.

20

*The Caterpillar
and the Butterfly*

The paradox of change is easy to understand and useful to work
on. It simply says that change takes place, not by carefully pro-
gramming the future, but by fully living the present. When I am
fully where I am, doing what I do and being what I am, my
organism senses by itself the next move and prepares me to
make it gently and effectively when the moment comes and nature in my soul awakens with the freshness of spring. When the
fruit is fully in contact with the tree, it grows and ripens day by
day till it knows its fullness and drops gratefully, in the sweet
perfection of its round softness, on the waiting hands of Mother
Earth. By plucking it before its time and forcing on it, through
manipulation and chemistry, an artificial ripening outside its
time, we destroy its sweetness and kill its taste. Change happens,
almost by itself, if we stay in contact and allow the vivifying sap
of divine grace to flow into us in the silence and peace in which
real growth takes place.

Our common mistake is to try to force change on ourselves.
We are impatient with our shortcomings, mortified by our blun-
ders, intolerant of our slowness. We want to progress, to improve, to reform, and set about it with noble zeal and purposeful
hurry. Plans and resolutions and targets and checkings. This

much to be achieved by that time, this bad habit to be uprooted and this beneficent trait to be acquired without delay. Plenty of good intentions and repeated efforts. And then repeated failures. The programmed changes are not forthcoming, the old habits remain, and the new practices do not last long. Back to the drawing board. For many years our lives are a succession of resolutions drafted and resolutions shelved. We have not learned the dynamics of change, and our unquestionable good will crashes against the hard reality of our stubborn nature. It is time we learn a little about the inner politics of the human mind. That may speed up our inward progress.

Change never occurs by decree. We cannot order it as we order an omelette or a pair of shoes. On the contrary, by marking a direction for our soul to follow, we unconsciously set in motion a hidden opposition, a current of inner dissent that will work underground to foil our conscious efforts toward the proposed goal. We all have found ourselves in the situation of wanting badly to remember a name in conversation, having it on the tip of our tongue, scouring every cell in our memory, and having to give up in despair . . . only to remember the name the moment the other person turns and goes and disappears out of hearing. The keen desire to remember can block the memory, just as the keen desire to change can block the way to change. This is the way our nature works, and this information can be of great help when we come to handling our lives and directing our progress. We know, at least, how not to set up blocks against ourselves.

We do not change by trying to be what we are not, but by being fully what we are. This is the secret. We do not change by looking at the future, but by living the present. When I am fully and generously all that I can and want to be in the present moment, I begin to feel inwardly ready to pass on to the next moment; when I am all I can be now, I spontaneously and obviously begin to be what I am to be next. The fullness of the present leads up by itself into the newness of the future. Today flowers into tomorrow when it is fully today, not when it pretends to be already tomorrow in impatient anticipation and undue haste. Thus change takes place precisely by not worrying about it, by not trying forcibly to bring it about, by not imposing it, by not seeking it. Let me be fully what I am today, and I shall wake up to a new world tomorrow.

An example: We know that a caterpillar turns into a chrysalis, and a chrysalis into a butterfly, which is a nature lesson of a wonderful change. Now, the caterpillar does not turn into a butterfly by *trying* to be a butterfly, by planning, scheming, endeavoring, or in any way contriving to be changed into a butterfly with colored wings and flying antennae. If it were to do that (as a man would surely do if he were in its place) it would only ruin its chances and spoil its future. A caterpillar becomes a butterfly by being a good, honest, healthy, reliable caterpillar; that is, by being fully and genuinely what it is now, not by trying to be what it is not. The better the caterpillar, the better the butterfly. The stronger the present, the brighter the future. The way for me to learn to fly one day is to walk firmly with my feet on the ground today. Nothing is achieved by dreaming and longing and craving and crying. Only by being fully what I am today can I get ready to be fully tomorrow what I can be tomorrow. My present stage fully lived is the best preparation for the next one. That is the wisdom of the caterpillar, and that is why it moves around contentedly at its leisurely pace. It trusts nature and it befriends time. It enjoys life crawling among leaves and branches, as one day it will enjoy life flying from flower to flower in the open sky. That is nature's kingdom.

And we are told that grace follows nature. The ways of grace, in its beauty and mystery, often mirror the workings of nature with its growth through the seasons and its flowering under the sun. All growth takes place at its heavenly appointed time under the guidance of the stars on God's good earth. We have faith in the universe because we have faith in God who created it, and we can trust its secret timings and its hidden tides. Spring will come in our souls if only we have the patience to last out the winter under the cold snow. A good winter is the best preparation for a good spring—both in the fields and in the soul.

Leonard Bernstein said a beautiful thing about Beethoven. He said first, in respectful criticism, that Beethoven was not a good melodist (he hummed goodhumoredly the first bars of the allegretto of the Seventh Symphony to prove his point); that he was not a good harmonist or even a good instrumentalist, and that he could not write a decent fugue in all his life, as much as he tried till he admitted defeat. Where was, then, the wonder of his music? Says Bernstein: in the "inevitability of the next note." Each note, each chord, each musical instant in Beethoven's compositions is so perfect, so pointed, so exact that it is asking with unavoidable peremptoriness for a concrete note and chord to follow, and no other one will do. In that perfection Beethoven stands alone. Each note is so total and unique in its lonely perfection that it can only be followed by another one equally suited to its own fleeting space with its own exclusive right. Each note reigns for an instant and names its heir in royal succession to a musical crown. Each note makes the next one inevitable. This is a beautiful thought and an inspiring image of the melody of life under the inspiration of grace. To live each moment with such fullness that the next one becomes obvious and inevitable in the artistic flow of a symphony of love. The change to the next note comes by itself out of the perfection of the present one. Again the future is spontaneously born out of the present.

The paradox of change is that it takes place by accepting and living what we are, not by endeavoring to be something else. Full contact with ourselves, full knowledge and acceptance of the present situation, full faith in nature and in grace, in ourselves and in God, full commitment to the present moment with all the zest of life and all the hope of the children of God. The way to the future is the enjoyment of the present.

A note of humor in this serious theme. Mulla Nasruddin was invited to go to England for the first time in his life, and prepared himself carefully for the important visit. He polished his English, learned British manners, practiced saying "sorry," "pardon," "excuse me," "thank you" at the least provocation, and endeavored to make himself familiar with all the ways and customs of the United Kingdom. While his preparation was going on, his friends learned one day with concern that the Mulla was in the hospital as he had been involved in a car accident. They went to see him, found him all wrapped in bandages, plaster, and dressings, and, after reassuring themselves that he would recover, asked him for his version of the accident. Nasruddin explained: "You know that I was getting ready to go to England, and I have landed in hospital instead. In fact that was the reason that got me here. I wanted to make myself familiar with all the British ways, and I heard that in England one drives on the left side of the road, not on the right as in the continent. I decided to get used to it well ahead of time so as to be able to drive without a hitch as soon as I got there. For that, I started practicing here, took the car on the left side of the road and drove on, till a lorry came right on against me, and you see the result."

That comes from bringing forcibly to the present what will in the course of things take place naturally in the future. The best preparation to drive on the left in England is to perfect one's driving on the right in the continent. Once in England, observation and a little practice will bring about the change as a matter of course; forcing the change too early leads only to a head-on collision. That explains so many accidents on the roads of life.

III

LIVING
THE
PRESENT

21

Do What You Do

When asked how the monks were to attain perfection, Buddha answered: "When the monk walks he is fully in his walking, when he stands he is fully in his standing, when he sits down he is fully in his sitting down, and when he lies down he is fully in his lying down. When he looks he is fully intent on looking, when he stretches out his hand he is intent on stretching out his hand, when he dresses he is intent on dressing, and, in the same way, when he eats, drinks, chews, or tastes, or performs any other action, he commits himself fully to what he is doing with perfect understanding of his action."

The program seems easy enough. Eat when you eat and walk when you walk. Is not that what we always do? Not quite. In fact, not at all. We rather do the opposite: We talk when we eat, think while we walk, and think again of something else while we were thinking the first thought. We are adept at mixing matters, at interrupting ourselves and keeping our minds far, far away from our hands and our feet. We hardly are where we are. We are expert at being where we are not, and at doing with our imaginations something different from what we are doing with our hands. *Age quod agis* was the old Latin precept: Do what you do. That is, do with all your mind, body, and soul whatever you happen to be doing at the moment, without distractions and without daydreams. We do understand the meaning of the precept and appreciate its wisdom; but we often find the daydreams sweeter. We have a squirrel within us that always keeps moving, keeps shifting, keeps jumping up and down as do those squirrels that own the garden around my room and peep through my window when I am writing, play with each other in endless merry-go-round, and nibble on my socks at night. Never steady, never in one place, never at rest. Sometimes they have to pay dearly for their flightiness. There is a public road with heavy traffic at the end of the garden, and the squirrels go through it in their usual wayward manner and zigzag course with sudden turn-abouts and back-jumps between speeding wheels and roaring engines. And I have seen more than once their lifeless little fur bodies pressed against the black tar of the road with an edge of blood. Death fixes finally to one place the little being that would not be steadied in its life.

Here in front of me is a man who has come to have a talk with me in private. He is sitting on the chair I have offered him. Or rather, he is not sitting, not at least in the common and restful sense of the word. He is precariously perched on the edge of the chair, leaning forward, about to lose his balance, tense and agitated. His body is not fully in the chair, as his mind is not fully in what he is saying. Poor contact with the chair bespeaks the poor contact he is making with reality, with his own situation, with the present moment. He is all worked up in telling trials of the past and fearing events of the future. He is not here. I can touch him if I stretch out my hand, but I cannot reach his mind because it is miles away. I ask him to be at ease, to relax and to sit comfortably. The chair is low and is curved backward for comfort. Significantly, he finds it difficult to accept my invitation to sit back and relax, though he smiles and tries to do so. He does sit deeper into the chair, but does not lean back, does not achieve contact with the back of the chair. The body reflects the attitude of the mind. Anxiety in the mind prevents relaxed contact in the body. And since the influence works both ways, there we have already in our hands an initial means to work toward peace in our minds. Physical contact with the furniture can mediate mental contact with reality. A relaxed body is the best preparation for a relaxed mind.

I have heard this only as a joke, but it is a good illustration of the same point: A man sits in a taxi, but sits only lightly without resting his full weight on the seat, in the erroneous belief that he will have to pay less that way. He does not know that the meter runs equally, whatever way he sits, and so he is only mortifying himself to no purpose. Let us sit in full comfort. The fare is the same.

Here is another common instance of being where we are not, and not being where we are. I am walking on a street when someone calls out my name. I look up in surprise. Where did he spring from? In fact he was walking toward me and I was looking in front of me but had not seen him till he literally was on me and called me by name. That is, I had seen him but had not noticed him; his image had certainly fallen on my retina but not on my awareness. He could have passed by my side, even touched me, and I would not have noticed him. I was perfectly blind because I was not where I was. I was in a hurry to get somewhere and my mind was racing to the spot while my feet still walked the street. I was not seeing people, however close they came to me, and so I did not recognize my friend. Once I had that experience with a little girl. She was coming, holding her mother's hand, from the other end of a long street, and when she came close I did see her and stopped to greet her. But then her mother told me, "She saw you right from the other end of the street when we turned the corner." The little girl had seen me much before I saw her. A child has pure eyes.

I found a very instructive instance of doing two things at the same time (and therefore neither of them well) in Mahatma Gandhi's correspondence. A little background is needed first. Gandhi popularized the use of the spinning wheel as a symbol of self-sufficiency and of India's independence from British rule, and he himself sat at the wheel daily for a good amount of time and expected his followers to do the same. His faithful personal secretary for many years was Mahadev Desai, and to him is addressed Gandhi's letter of November 13, 1930, a letter which must have certainly surprised him. Mahadev was in jail, like many Indian patriots in those days, and from jail he had written to Gandhi that he spent most of his time at the spinning wheel, and that now he had found another useful occupation to fill the time of the enforced leisure. There was another political prisoner in the same jail, a man called Abba Saheb, who knew French, and since that language would be useful for Gandhi's secretary in his international contacts, Mahadev had begun to take French lessons from Abba Saheb. To make even better use of the time, in full Gandhian spirit, Mahadev had put the two things together, and learned French while spinning at the wheel. He had told Gandhi about it in his letter, hoping thereby to win his approval and rejoice his heart. He did not. His behavior greatly displeased Gandhi, who said so in his answer. "I am distressed," he wrote, "at the news about yourself. How can you, who are so close to me, have misunderstood me so badly? How is it you have not yet understood the message of the spinning wheel? Whatever we do requires our full attention, and do not think that because spinning is a material occupation it can be done mechanically and without care. Whatever we do has to be done well, with all our mind and all our heart. One thing at a time, and every work done to perfection. Study French by all means, but stop the spinning wheel while you learn French. Do you not remember having [discussed] with me what Romain Rolland says in his book on Beethoven about his concentration while playing the piano? And is the spinning wheel any less important than the piano? I feel pained to see that you have not yet realized the holiness of the spinning wheel, as indeed of everything we do."

Gandhi's disciples today seem to have forgotten that teaching. For instance, it is common practice in Gandhian institutions to keep working at the spinning wheel while listening to a lecture. It is a trying experience for the lecturer, as I know from my own experience. I feel quite uncomfortable speaking to a hundred people who, while sitting on the floor, keep turning their spinning wheels, drawing the thread, coiling the yarn, feeding the spindle in obvious concentration on what they are doing and oblivious to what I am saying. The impression I get is that they consider my lecture useless anyhow, so they want to put the time to some good use by manufacturing something. Fine, but then why did they call me in the first place? Shortly after I read Gandhi's letter I was invited to one such institution presided over by none other than Mahadev Desai's own son. I was to deliver the annual address on Founder's Day. I did so, and Gandhi's secretary's son listened to my speech sitting on the floor by my side and turning the spinning wheel without a break. I did not tell him about Gandhi's letter to his father.

22

Here and Now

Be what you are. Do what you do. The following case, though extreme, actually took place, and I know well the person involved in it. He and others in a small therapy group each had been asked to improvise ten sentences beginning with "Here and now I. . . ." This man volunteered to do so, and after two or three innocuous sentences came out with the following gem: "Here and now I . . . was yesterday quarreling with my wife at home." Honest man he was. He had been so deeply affected by the domestic quarrel that today and in the group he was still living that unhappy experience with such realism that his today was still yesterday, and the hall his home. He had not closed the incident in his mind, and so he literally did not know where he was. He was still turning over in his mind the previous day's event, and the stubborn memory prevented him from moving ahead in his day. The unfinished situation, the open wound, the unsettled account: Few things hinder our contact with reality more than the situations that hang on without closure. So long as we do not satisfactorily finish a chapter in our private autobiography, we are not in a position to start a new one.

Our thoughts, whether in study, in conversation, or in prayer, do not easily follow a continuous course; and they interrupt themselves in random desultoriness. A student complains that he cannot concentrate on his studies, and a religious person asks for guidance on how to resist distractions during prayer. Even in ordinary conversation we often miss something that has been said and must ask the other person to repeat it simply because we were distracted. "Distraction" is in itself a rather forbidding word: Dis-traction means literally "tearing apart." When we are distracted we tear ourselves apart, we pull ourselves to pieces, we cease to be whole, to be one, to be sane. To be distracted means that we are divided, that we are not fully where we are, that we have lost contact. We are acting out yesterday's incomplete situations, or we are projecting tomorrow's worries onto today's screen. Either way we are split, and thus fail to live the fullness of life at the only moment we can live it, which is the here and now.

Psychologists define the neurotic as a "self-interrupter," and I am afraid most of us would generously qualify for the label under that definition. On the other hand, we can use those interruptions to know ourselves better. Every distraction, whether in conversation or in prayer, is the loose end of an unfinished situation that is asking to be closed in order to allow us to enjoy the next one. I had one experience that enabled me to understand bodily and painfully in my flesh the harm that loose ends may cause. I had been operated upon, and the wound did not heal in the expected time. The surgeon tried several medications, all to no effect. The wound would not heal. Finally it had to be fully reopened, and then it was found that the inner stitches had not been properly cut, and their ends were dangling freely, not allowing the wound to close. They were then cut, and the wound healed up, leaving an ugly scar as a protest for the careless handling. We carry many open wounds on us because the stitches had not been properly made. Open wounds mean continued suffering and exposure to danger. And all unnecessarily. A good surgeon does not leave loose ends.

An introspective writer said about himself: I always think of the right answer . . . when I am going down the stairs. This is also a common experience with most of us. We had a discussion, an argument, or just a conversation in which ideas were exchanged and opinions expressed, and we do think of the proper opinion and the exact phrase, but only when the meeting is over and we are descending the steps of the house. Then comes the witty answer, the neat repartee, the opportune quotation that would have closed the other person's mouth and established our triumph in dialectics. But it comes too late, and we can only tell it to ourselves and repeat it uselessly with the pull of frustration and self-recrimination for not having thought of it at the proper time. I should have told him this! Or, on the contrary, I should not have told him that! A word said or unsaid that tortures me now because it did not come out when it should have, or it did when it should have not. Regret and anger, and the small open wound chafing all through the day. Because I did not live the present in full at that moment, I cannot live it any more in the ensuing time. Lack of contact on one occasion results in increased lack of contact for the next. The sooner we stop the chain reaction, the better.

I had one such experience on a flight of steps. A girl in my mathematics class at college had obtained the first prize in an elocution competition. I saw her come down the steps while I was going up to take my class, we crossed at the middle of the stairs, and I turned to her as we crossed and told her, "Congratulations for your trophy!" She did not react and continued her way down while I went up. When I reached the top of the stairs she suddenly turned up and shouted toward me: "Thank you! Sorry I didn't notice you at first!" And we both went our ways. Fortunately the stairs had been long enough to allow for her reaction time, and we both enjoyed the pleasant awkwardness of the delayed response. Her mind was on something else, she did not expect me to know about her success or to mention it at a chance crossing, and so, though my words reached her ears clearly, they took some time to reach her conscious mind and allow for a reaction. We do hear and know and understand and have the right answer to the right question, and the proper reaction to the incoming stimulus, but there are blocks along the way, and the message takes time to reach the brain, and often it reaches too late. The other person is gone, the stairs have come to an end, the occasion has passed. And our reaction loses its freshness. If that girl had thanked me the next day, I would have felt embarrassed. A twenty-four-hour overdue "thank you" is a poor "thank you."

And yet that is what our reactions often are: slow and over-due. Those blocks within us prevent us from being truly our-selves, from being fully engaged in what we are and responding therefore with all the spark of our intellect and all the warmth of our feelings. The simple art of closing every door we open eludes us, and we leave behind us on our way a trail of open doors that keep banging in the wind and disturbing our forward march. An unpleasant experience leaves behind it a trace of regret for hav-ing been trapped into it, and of anger against all concerned, beginning with oneself. And a pleasurable experience leaves the desire to prolong it, to repeat it, to recall it again and again in such a way that it does not give pleasure anymore; this is because it has passed and thus prevents us from taking pleasure in the present, which has been overshadowed by the memory of the past. These blocks undermine our vitality and destroy our spon-taneity.

One way to uncover those blocks is, as I have just mentioned, to follow the train of our distractions. They lead us to the hid-den anxieties and frustrations that put up those blocks in fear and revenge, and facing them helps us to remove them. I watch myself as I am engaged in some activity that requires continued attention. I am reading a book, writing a letter, listening to a lecture, following a conversation, praying. Before long my mind is somewhere else. Where? I follow the thought; that is, I allow the distraction to continue along its way, and soon I notice, not without some amusement, that a new distraction has arisen within the distraction leading me away in another direction. I follow the direction. It can be fun. Something similar to the free association of a Freudian analyst. If the mind brings up something, there is a reason for it. Face it. Perhaps it is a nonassimilated experience, or a feared task. There is a residue in the mind that has not been cleared, and that therefore causes the obstruction or the deviation. The discovery of the obstacle is the first step to its removal. Let us get on with it.

A young man has come to see me and talk with me about his life. After a while I notice that I am distracted. I am not listening to him. I have lost track of what he is saying. I check myself. I am not precisely in a hurry. I have given him time, and he has full right to make use of it. I had kept myself free and shown my willingness to talk with him. I pride myself on being a fairly good listener, expressing interest and eliciting trust. Yet nothing of the kind is happening today. I am hopelessly distracted and longing for the interview to be over. Why? I know now. I have realized, from what the young man has said so far, that I have no answer for his problem. When he finishes talking I shall have to say a few useless things, try to console him in any way I can, and let him go without satisfaction on his part or mine. That is why I do not want to listen to him. It is not that his story lacks interest, but that my skills fall short of his case. I feel uneasy and unhappy, and my mind finds escape in getting distracted. I see it plainly while the young man is still talking. And then a very significant thing happens. I have not yet spoken, I have not yawned or looked at my watch or given any open sign of being inattentive. Yet the young man interrupts his story, looks up at me, and says disarmingly: "I am boring you with my story, isn't that it?" Somehow the message has gotten through. He has sensed my lack of interest, though he does not know the reason. My distraction has given me away. It is only left for me to uncover the reason and own up to it. He understands. My distraction has taught me my limitation.

23

May I Tape Your Lecture?

When I am about to begin a talk in public, or a more or less formal discussion with a group of interested people, there is always someone or other who is considerate enough to ask the question: "Do you mind if I tape the session?" There are in fact several tape-recorders in evidence, though not all their owners have thought of asking for permission, some because they take it for granted, and others because they are afraid it will be refused. So when one explicitly asks the question, they all take their machines in hand, ready to withdraw them if I show displeasure. The fact is that I do not care, and I let them know so in clear terms to relieve them. Some even take the trouble to mention that they are not taping the proceedings for themselves but for a friend who wanted to come and has not been able to do so, and has made them promise they will bring back the precious words permanently recorded for his or her spiritual benefit. Others do not trust themselves to remember everything, are afraid of missing some invaluable remark, and want to make sure it will be preserved for them safely in the lasting guarantee of the faithful tape. In any case the machines are switched on, and the red eyes of their recording lights keep blinking in unison with the volume of my voice and remind me that I am talking.

I keep talking, and well into the proceedings I take my little revenge on the machines and their owners. I say something first gently so that most people do not realize what I have said, least of all those who are taping the talk. Then I say it bluntly so that nobody can fail to understand the point, but by then the machines have been running a long time and it would be awkward to stop them halfway, so that the eager scribes just become embarrassed, smile and feel silly, and the talk continues and the machines keep blinking. The point I make by doing this is that, because they know the talk is in the tape, they may forget to record it in their brains. Since it is safely preserved in the cassette, they feel they can afford to be distracted, to miss details, indeed to miss the whole talk, since they shall always have time to listen to it at leisure on the tape-recorder. If there were to be no record, and if this interested them, they would be on their toes, pay full attention, grasp every idea and try to remember every example. It would be their only chance, and they would make the best of it. It would be an experience, an activity, a learning situation. But now they know that the machine is working. Its red eye keeps blinking. Every word is there. So they relax, lose attention, get distracted, and the machine is good enough to click its auto-stop when the tape comes to an end so that they wake up, turn on another tape, and relax again. It is all there. They need not worry. It is a new tape, and the recording will be clear and distinct. Let the talk go on.

Yes, it is all there. But it is not *here*. That is, it is in the machine but not in the brain. It is in the tape, and, therefore, not in the mind. Since the tape-recorder is doing the listening for me, I can neglect my own listening. And once the talk is there, since I know I can always listen to it, I shall never do it. Why to hurry? It is always available and can wait for another occasion. It waits. The tape rests at ease, and the talk may not be listened to at all. When it was delivered it was not listened to because it was going to be listened to in the leisure of the tape, and when it is in the tape it is not played because it has lost its freshness. This may happen, and the tape-recorder may become an obstacle to plain and direct listening.

I know because it happens to me. I often listen to music on the radio while I am working. I listen with greater or lesser attention to pieces I know, and occasionally I prick up my ears when a composition is announced in which I am particularly interested. Then I promptly introduce a tape into my radio cassette-recorder and tape the piece. And then a curious thing happens. I do not pay attention to the piece while it is being played and recorded. Since I know that it is going to be permanently with me and I shall be able to listen to it whenever I want, I get distracted and pay no attention to it. Thus the paradoxical situation obtains that I listen with greater attention to music in which I am less interested, because I am not recording it and so I instinctively make the best of the passing chance; whereas I pay less attention to the music I like more because, since I have recorded it, I know it will always be with me. And then again, once it is recorded and kept among my cassettes, sometimes a very long time passes without my listening to it, for the same reason. Since it is always available it is never used. The value, urgency, and keenness of a unique firsthand listening at the unique opportunity can be spoiled by the deceptive convenience of the ready recording.

Once Barry Stevens listened to a talk by Fritz Perls, and reflected after it: "I have just listened to a talk by Fritz. I do not remember anything he said; if you ask me for any of the points made or the arguments offered I cannot tell them, and if I had to pass an examination on it I would get a zero. But the talk is all over me, I know that it is there deep in my system, and, the moment I need it, it will come up and be ready for me to use." This is a beautiful experience. She has listened with all her organism, mind and body, ears, brains, skin and bones. She has opened herself to the communication, has literally taken in all that has been said without any distraction of taking notes or running tapes; she trusts in her own nature and knows that the secret files will be ready for use the moment they are needed. Because she has listened in freedom she will remember at ease. On the contrary, the person who listens to a lecture with a view to passing an examination on it will certainly pass the examination if he or she tries, but will not have the knowledge ready for life in his or her inmost self. Degrees do not qualify one for living.

Taking notes during a lecture is slightly better than recording it on tape, as it involves some personal activity—understanding, summarizing, jotting down—but it is also essentially a distraction as it distorts the present into the future, and the hand is writing one idea while the ears are listening to the next one, with the brain torn between the ear and the hand, spoiling all chances to assimilate the new thoughts in peace. Lectures are for listening, and textbooks for reading. The anxiety to record the spoken message on paper or on tape takes away its freshness, vitality, and perenniality. Everything that wounds the present, wounds life.

I learned that lesson the hard way early in my student days. The fashion among eager students for the priesthood in those days was to build up a personal file with all sorts of quotations, summaries, stories, and examples for use in future teaching and preaching, as remote preparation for our priestly ministry. There could be no better intention in our effort which also implied a good amount of hard work. Soon, however, the innate tendency to provide for the future overstepped all bounds, and our files became our main activity. A wise teacher saw the excess and cut it rather drastically. He ordered us to bring all our precious files, piled them up together in the garden, and made a bonfire of them. We obediently accepted the loss, almost as a trial of faith. In fact it was simple common sense. We were busy gathering material which would be of no use to us years later, given the way tastes change and given the gap between our present fantasies and future reality. And that frenzy was getting in the way of our true formation, of our tasting, enjoying, and digesting the material we were handling then. The best preparation for the future is the proper use of the present. That was the meaning of the timely bonfire.

24

The Sweet Berry

Living the present includes, of course, reasonably foreseeing and providing for the future. Whenever I talk about this theme (which is quite often, as it is my favorite one), someone or other will unfailingly object, saying—often with a deriding tone—that it is all very fine to talk about living in the present, but if I want to travel tomorrow I have to think of it and make a reservation today; if I want to give a lecture I have to prepare it well in advance; and if I want to retire comfortably in my old age I have to begin saving now. I cannot fly by cheerfully going to the airport, asking nonchalantly the first pilot I meet on the premises whether he is going to my destination, and proposing to join him without more ado if he is flying there. That is not the way things work, my opponent reminds me, and so all this talk of living in the present is all very nice, and very impractical as well. Just as one cannot forget the past, one cannot in any way neglect the future if one is to live a reasonable life. Sensible people think of the future, and that is why insurance companies thrive. Empty philosophies do not make for a secure and respectable life.

I often notice that such an objection is made with a patronizing tone, and sometimes even with a latent aggressiveness; and I interpret that aggressiveness as the reluctance our minds have to live in the present. It is a stubborn, irrational, universal reluctance. As soon as we try to fix our mind on the present, it bolts and rears, and justifies its escape with a thousand reasons. People resist bravely any attempt to bring them to face the present, which means in fact to face themselves, since the present is the only situation in which they are as they are, not as they were or as they want to be. We do not like to see ourselves in the mirror, and so our mind instinctively resists any attempt to bring it to the present. An aging king in Indian legend ordered all mirrors in his palace to be destroyed. We too want to avoid the reflection of the present so as not to see our faces as they are.

Whatever has to be done in the present for the reasonable care of the future is part of the present, and as such is no exception and no distraction. Of course we have to plan and foresee, and to make reservations beforehand and to buy insurance if so desired. There is nothing wrong with that. The danger comes when we overload the present with thoughts of the future. And the greatest abuse comes when we do that and we call it wisdom, and consider as models those who behave accordingly. Our training has been biased in that direction, which makes it all the more difficult for us to recover the sense of the present. In a society that prizes providence for the future it is not easy to revalue the present.

When I was at school I had to memorize La Fontaine's fables as part of my French lessons. I can still recite that tale about the cicada and the ant, with its praises for the industriousness of the ant that works hard throughout the summer to ensure that it will have food in the winter, and the rather merciless condemnation of the cicada (or grasshopper) for its carefree singing during summer and its subsequent freezing and hunger under the winter snow. Today I remember the verses, but think otherwise. For one thing, the fable is not true to fact. Grasshoppers do not starve in winter, and nature has its ways of looking after different species in different ways. For another thing, the ant does not look to be a particularly happy insect, and its life of permanent drudgery is not precisely suitable as a model for human life. And for yet another thing, if the grasshopper knows how to sing and feels like doing so in the sunny hours of the summer days, it is welcome to do so, and all the fields around will be grateful for it. The grasshopper enjoys the present and invites all to do the same, while the ant is all future and thinks only of how to survive underground when the going gets tough on the surface. And the fable condemns the grasshopper—that is, condemns the joys of the present while it commends the provision for the future. This is a lesson inculcated in our minds from a tender age, and we never seem to outgrow the teaching. We feel guilty when we sing in summer. (Ernest Hemingway criticized La Fontaine precisely for this.)

There is an ancient parable recorded in both Indian and Chinese scriptures. It goes like this: A wayfarer along a dangerous route slips, and is about to fall from a precipice into a deep abyss when he manages to get hold of the branch of a bush on the cliff's edge and hangs onto it. In that precarious situation he looks up and sees a lion and a tiger ready to devour him if he dares to climb back onto level ground; what is worse, two mice, one black and one white, are gnawing at the root of the bush with rather dangerous efficiency. He then looks down and sees a steep fall, a crocodile-infested river, and murderous rapids up to a waterfall without bottom. To complete the scene, vultures hover around him ready to finish the job if the other characters do not. A rather thorough predicament for a naive wanderer. At that moment he notices a ripe berry on the shrub, takes it, puts it in his mouth, and . . . it tastes so sweet!

I once saw a life-sized reproduction of this scene in a religious exhibition organized by a fervent Hindu sect. The awesome episode, all done in plaster of Paris and gaudy colors, was the center of the exhibition, and the lesson it was meant to teach was imprinted in large characters all over the landscape. Foolish man! His life is but a passing instant amidst deadly dangers; he may die at any moment and be thrown into the bottomless abyss of eternal punishment; he should think of his plight and turn to prayer and virtue to redeem somehow the misery of his existence . . . but all he does in his foolishness is to taste the passing sweetness of a perishable pleasure! All worldly pleasures are like the insignificant berry in the treacherous shrub. Give up all pleasures, meditate on the fickleness of life, turn to God and do penance! The madness of man in the pursuit of earthly pleasures is represented by the senseless behavior of the irresponsible wayfarer in the face of death. A small berry is enough to entice him! Can there be something more foolish than that?

Visitors to the exhibition were duly impressed by the visual sermon, and left the stand in thoughtful silence. I also left it in an introverted mood, but the reason was different. All my sympathies were with the victim of the parable. I think that in taking the berry and enjoying it, he did the only sensible thing that could be done in the circumstances. If I cannot get out of this mess, let me at least enjoy the one thing that is within reach, and we shall see later how the situation develops. He could not very well handle the lion and the tiger, the crocodiles and the vultures, nor even the two meddlesome mice in their unpleasant officiousness. He could only taste the berry, and this he proceeds to do with courageous simplicity and a humble touch of healthy realism. My heartfelt admiration for his presence of mind! The interesting point is that this is precisely the moral of the original story. In its original setting, this story was meant to emphasize the importance of the present moment, to teach the essential lesson of living in the present without fears or distractions of past or future, however formidable these may seem. Do the only thing you can do, enjoy the little berry, symbol and image of the present moment—and trust that if you quietly make of this moment the only use you can profitably make of it, the next moment will also offer its fruit, and life will be lived from moment to moment in its unpredictable newness and ever-surprising adventure. That is, in fact, how the story continues. While the man munches his berry, the lion kills the tiger, and the tiger the lion; in their fight they shake the bush and the two mice fall into the abyss to be devoured by the crocodiles; the vultures then rescue the wanderer who goes happily on his way, admiring the view of the rapids and the waterfall from the top. It would have been a pity if he had missed the sweetness of the berry.

25

Leave No Footprints

Hindu mythology explains that there are three ways to distinguish a god from an ordinary mortal when the gods choose to walk the earth in human guise. To all appearances they look like ordinary men and women, and nothing in the way they walk, talk, and carry themselves would single them out as visitors from another world. But there are three signs that one can observe if one pays attention, and any one of them gives away the divine character of the person in whom it is detected. Gods and goddesses on earth do not blink their eyelids, they cast no shadows and leave no footprints. These traits identify them to the careful observer.

They are truly divine traits. To leave no footprints; to tread lightly on life. To cast no shadow; not to project or prolong the necessary contact with life in any way or any direction, in front or behind, in the looming darkness of a distorted ghost. And never to blink, never to lose eye contact with the world all around—be it even for the fleeting instant of a momentary wink. The sign of wisdom. The living presence. Being fully on earth for all practical purposes, but detached, untrammeled, unbound. Leaving no trace of their earthly passage, no memories, no ties. Nothing to anchor their past or condition their future. Like the passing of the wind on the treetops in the early hours of a spring day.

To leave no footprints. Even the Bible ascribes that ethereal quality to the God of Israel in astonished testimony: "His footsteps did not appear!" (Ps. 76:20). God performs his wonders, and leaves no trace. Even the mighty works of his extended arm are performed with such ease that they leave no mark. And men wonder about the workings of God.

The trouble with leaving footprints on the sand is not only that the sand is marked by the foot, but the foot by the sand. Grains of the sands of time stick to our feet and lodge themselves between our toes, and so we carry our past with us, and after a time it hurts and weighs on us and slows down our pace. To walk through life without leaving footprints is a divine art that brings peace and joy to the foot that walks. To reach everywhere and stick nowhere, to come and to go, to enter gently and to depart lightly. Not to burden the mind with the baggage of memories, attachments, resentments, regrets, but to keep it open and free so it can move with ease along the paths of life. To leave no markings on the mind.

It is not easy to come out of every situation in life without being marked by it, without its sticking to us in one way or other to the detriment of our forward march. We do not come out clean from the encounters, the episodes, the trials and the pleasures of our complicated lives. Every event leaves its trace on us, and the layers of the past soon cover the freshness of the present. If only we knew how to come clean out of every occasion, we would move through life with far greater grace and joy.

How, then, to come out clean from every occasion? The answer is simple, almost tautological, and involves us in a teasing vicious circle. That is why it is no answer at all, as there are no final answers and no magic clues to the problems of the mind. It is only a way of saying the same thing all over again in a slightly different way with the hope that an atmosphere be built up around us and the breathing of new air may awaken the mind in its day to a new freshness and a new vitality. This is, then, the mirror answer to the demanding question, or, putting it more gently, the provisional explanation of our permanent quandary: Why do we not fully come out of the events in our life? We do not fully come out of the events, big or small, in our daily lives because we do not fully enter into them. The contact is not full for a start, and so it cannot be full at the end either. A half-hearted entry makes for a half-hearted exit. And, of course, to complete the circle, why do we not get fully into an event? Because we did not fully get out of the previous one. We may now choose at which point we want to break the circle.

I do not entrust myself fully to life in its day-to-day manifestations because I do not possess myself fully, I do not know myself, I do not understand myself, I do not trust myself. I am afraid of suffering, and I am afraid of pleasure, as I have not yet learned how to enjoy things with a good conscience. I am dissatisfied with myself, anxious, impatient, nervous. How can I get into anything with all my heart when my heart is divided and each part is going its own way? And above and in between all these things I detect a tendency in myself that foils all my attempts at recovering my fullness and putting it into play. That tendency is sheer laziness, a kind of stinginess of the mind—the reluctance of my mind to put itself out in earnest even when it knows that would be for its own good. There is a kind of hidden miserliness in human nature that prevents me from employing myself fully in any event, that counts the cost of everything and wants me to save my energies for future emergencies, not realizing that the only way to reinforce the powers of the soul is to use them in full. Everything matters. Everything I do is important, because it is me. There is no small event in life, no negligible occasion, no minor opportunity. All that happens to me requires the whole of me, and by holding back and letting only half of me into the fray I only do harm to myself and stunt my growth. Lack of generosity with life is the reason I do not allow myself to develop as I know I could.

I am to preside at a solemn Eucharist tomorrow before a large congregation, and I have planned to prepare it painstakingly—to study the gospel of the day, put together carefully an inspiring homily, think in advance of the prayers, introductions, invitations for the key moments of the ceremony, and make sure it will be a rewarding experience for all those who take part in it. They are an enlightened congregation, and they will be able to appreciate my handling of the sacred mysteries. Everything will be carefully thought out. But then, before I begin my preparation, I am informed that there has been a change of plans: The solemn Eucharist will not be held and there will be an ordinary service that only a few people will attend. My first reaction, when informed of the change, is to drop my preparation. I will improvise a few words as I go along in the ceremony, and that will be all. Why make any special preparation, take any particular interest when only a few people are going to be present? A waste of energy. Let me save my strength, my time, and my thoughts for another occasion. No special effort for tomorrow.

But then I check myself. Why am I devaluating tomorrow's event? Simply because fewer people will be coming? My performance, then, depends on numbers? But my performance means myself, my worth, my person. If I put myself into something, I want to put myself into it heart and soul, with all my interest and all my strength. Whether a dozen people attend or a hundred, I am the same and the Eucharist is the same. I am going to take pains and prepare and reflect, and I will face the small congregation with light in my eyes and warmth in my heart, and I will make the celebration an enriching experience for them, because only then will it be such an experience for me—a full engagement, a worthy task in which I will get fully involved without any misgivings, any curtailments, or any stinginess. There I go, the whole of me, keeping nothing back. I do keep a sense of proportion, of course, between work and the preparation for it, and give more time to more important work; but the attitude, the readiness, the commitment have to be the same in every case because whatever the work to be done it is I who do it, and I do not split myself into parts or dispense myself in portions. I have full interest in everything I do. That makes for satisfaction, and consequently for greater facility in passing on to the next experience with a clean slate.

This is the flow of life, the "continuum of awareness," the precise contact. The concept of "closure," of completion, of finality applied to each work, to each situation and each instant in life. The "contact-withdrawal rhythm" that marks the trail of the wise person on earth.

> He walked through the forest, and not one leaf stirred:
> he entered the waters, and no ripples were formed.
> *Bankei*

> Feet in the jungle that leave no mark!
> Eyes that can see in the dark—the dark!
> *Rudyard Kipling*

Life without footprints, without a shadow, without blinking.

> One moment past
> Our bodies cast
> No shadow on the plain.
> *Rudyard Kipling**

I am going to carefully keep watching the people around me day by day for the telling signs, to see when I am privileged to meet a god or a goddess.

The Jungle Book, Avenal Books, 1982, pp. 18, 130.

26

Two Cups of Tea

I learned an important lesson one day. I learned that two cups of
tea are never the same. I once saw a book with the title *Two
Hundred Ways of Making Tea*. Quite a reminder for those who
believe tea to be a monotonous beverage. (I can hardly stand the
brew, but I have succumbed to the Indian custom, and take it
obediently without flinching whenever the hospitality rubrics
ask for it, which is about half a dozen times a day.) My experience, in any case, went that day far beyond the different ways of
putting together the leaves and the water. It went on to teach me
something important about myself and about the ways we subconsciously lower our capacity to enjoy life. This is the way I
learned it.

I was staying for a few days in the house of a friend in the
Indian city where I live. The first morning he unobtrusively
watched my goings for a while; and when, in the early hours, I
sat down cross-legged at floor level to begin my morning work,
he appeared silently at the door with a tray in his right hand,
and two cups of tea on the tray. The day in India begins with
tea, and he had had the thoughtful courtesy to bring me in
person the "drink of the gods" and accompany me in the ritual.
He gave me one cup, took the other, and sat also cross-legged in
front of me, still silent. I put aside my writing implements, took
the cup he offered me, and remained in silent communion with

him. We began to sip our tea slowly, unhurriedly, almost solemnly, letting the gentle warm touch on our lips announce to
every cell in our bodies that the taste had arrived. The morning
tea is the official opening of the new day.

After a while he began to talk slowly, and soon the mood of
dawn, the silence of the hour, the bond of friendship, the sacra-
mental witness of the tea taken together led him on to subjects
grounded in intimacy and personal revelation; and I responded
with the best of my feelings in parallel surrender to the mutual
trust in the very depths of our souls. Moments of private wonder, of confident reaching-out, of living one experience in two
souls. He went deeper and deeper in his spiral of personal re-
membrances, I nodded or spoke in an occasional monosyllable
to signal my closeness, and both of us let long silences mark the
shared rhythm of our increasing togetherness.

The minutes went by. The tea in our cups grew lower and
colder. The light of the day increased visibly while we talked.
The matter of our talk also was by itself drawing to a close, and
we said the last word when we took the last sip together. The tea
was over. The conversation was over. We still remained a few
moments seated silently in each other's presence. Then he stood
up, took the cup from me, placed it on the tray together with
his, bowed gracefully and left me to my work. I took my pen and
began writing in the glow left by his presence. It had been a
momentous encounter.

The day then went its way. My first day in his house. The
morning meal, our going out to our separate work, the return in
the evening, the night meal, the meeting with the family, the
playing with the children, the joyful moments of their uninhib-
ited laughter, and the reluctant turning to work again—they to
their school homework, and I to my writing. Then the blessing
of the night, the turning in one by one, the last word before the
white silence of the fresh bedsheets. The rest between two days.

The second morning dawned and the second day began with

the familiarity of our once-rehearsed routine. I sat down to my work, and my host, at the same time, appeared at my door with the tray in his hand and the two cups of tea. The previous day's scene was to be enacted again. I took my cup thoughtfully, and warmed up inside me for the encounter. The memory of yesterday was fresh in my mind, and I wanted to live up to it. Yesterday our private tea ceremony had proved deeply satisfying, and today it could not be less. As I began to taste my tea I reflected inside me that yesterday it was he who had started the intimate sharing, and so today it was my turn. I had to find something important to say, something personal, something moving, to match his performance of yesterday. I started casting about in my mind for some such opening, at first gently and then, as the moments went by and nothing worthwhile occurred to me, somewhat nervously. I had to come up with something of note, something well said to draw out our feelings and coax our dialogue. I could not let this occasion slip by without making the most of it, as I knew it could be done and had been done yesterday. I would never forgive myself if, considering the few days I was going to be here, I let this precious opportunity pass without bringing it to its full value. The level of the tea in the cup had begun to go down. What could I do before it was too late?

Then in the midst of my inner agitation I had a moment of calm. I had the good sense to look at him as he sat in front of me holding his cup in his hand, and I saw that his face was calm and composed. There was no anxiety on it, no expectation, no demand that I should come up with an intimate confidence, that I should speak at all. He was just taking his tea in thoughtful recollection, in silent communion, in self-fulfilled presence. There was no need to talk. There was no need to think, to be agitated, to worry. I calmed down. I let his silence touch me. I recovered the taste of the tea. I relaxed. I let the moments pass at their unhurried pace. Then two sparrows entered the room and filled it with their twittering and their play. We watched them in quiet pleasure. We finished our tea in unison. We still remained seated for a while. Then he stood up, took my empty cup, and spoke for the first time. He said, "Today the sparrows will keep you company." And he left me with them.

He left me with my thoughts too. And my thoughts were just then a flurry of clear emotions. I saw it all. The mistake I had been about to make, and the redeeming awareness that had saved the day. The mistake was to want to repeat yesterday's experience today. Yesterday the morning tea had been a memorable experience, so today it had to be too. Yesterday he had spoken, so today I had to do it. I had the pattern, the model, the precedent. I knew what the morning tea with my friend had to be. I would not fail. I knew what was expected of me, and I would make good. I can talk intimately when I so choose, and today I will do it in response to my friend's having done it yesterday. I have a debt to pay, an account to settle. I have to make a success out of today's tea, and I will do it even if I have to strain every nerve and tap every resource for it. I was bent on repeating the past. And repeating the past is the sure way to ruin the present. I had almost succeeded in spoiling the second day's tea by making it a mimicry of the first.

And then I woke up. The presence of my friend had brought me back to reality and to the realization that there was nothing special to be done except letting things be what they were. And then things, by themselves, were new and fresh and different. Today's tea was to be different from yesterday's. Yesterday it was in dialogue, today in silence. Yesterday there were words, today, the twittering of sparrows. Yesterday we had exchanged ideas, today we exchanged looks. And today's tea had been also wonderful in its own way, precisely because it had been entirely different from yesterday's.

Two cups of tea are never the same. Even if they have been

made by the same person in the same kettle in the same way, they are different. That was the very important lesson I had to learn. Important to me, as I have to drink about six cups of tea every day.

27

Every Time We Meet . . .

If the tea made by the same person in the same way is different on two different days, how much more so the person who makes it! He or she also changes from moment to moment, and therefore from day to day, and the recognition of this simple fact can go a long way to bring liveliness and joy to our relationships. In fact it is the change in the person that is reflected in the change in the tea, and this makes every morning different and every encounter unique. There is such a richness in the human person that every facet is new and every spark a surprise. The art is to allow ourselves to be surprised by people we have known for years and who we meet daily and take for granted in the routine of a colorless monotony. Perhaps the greatest sin one person can commit against another is to take him for granted. That robs him of his personality, his newness, his life. That is murder in the mind, it is not allowing my brother to be himself, and therefore not allowing him to be. I have frozen him in the files of my past, and have made him into a comfortable memory, easy to deal with along predictable patterns. Very convenient for business. And very unfair for life. My brother is alive and he fits into no patterns and must be allowed to show me today the face he wants to show. It is a crime to make him into a mummy.

George Bernard Shaw said once: "My tailor is the wisest of all persons who come to see me. Every time he comes, he takes new measurements." True wisdom indeed. The man has changed. Not only height and waist, but gait and bearing and the minimal adjustments in limb and joint that change with the days and that make for the exact fitting of a new suit of clothes. No tailor who respects himself will cut new cloth on old measurements. Take the trouble and measure the man. Only then can you hold the scissors and shape the suit.

Measure the person anew. Look at your brother with a fresh eye. Do not classify him, do not label him as though he were a biological specimen. Do not dismiss him in your mind telling yourself, "I know what he is going to say, I know what he thinks and I know how he reacts; I can spare myself the trouble of asking him, because he has always been the way I know him and will always be. Not in vain have we been so many years together." Give him a chance. And, above all, give yourself the chance of looking at things and at persons anew. You are the loser when you take the other for granted and refuse to look into his or her eyes today. You miss then the newness of life in things and in persons all around you, and condemn yourself to a humdrum existence. To come alive ourselves we must allow all men and women around us to come alive too.

One day I was going to meet my classes in the university as on any other day of the year. In the mathematics department I found my best friend and colleague, and, with the daily familiarity that marked our friendship, I jumped without introduction into the telling of a funny incident that had happened to me that morning and that I thought would amuse him as it had amused me. "Can you imagine what happened to me just now!" And I went with full zest into the detailed narrative of the amusing story. I finished it in a loud monologue, and waited for his reaction. There was none. I then looked at his face, which is what I should have done first. He was obviously worried and in pain. I felt sorry I had spoken at all. I lowered my voice and said gently, very gently, with contrition in my tone: "What has happened? Tell me if you don't mind." He explained. "My son. You know him. He developed a very high fever last night. He has been admitted to the hospital, and I am coming from there. I am worried, because we don't have a diagnosis yet. Could you arrange for my classes to be covered today? I would like to get back to my son at once." I assured him it would be done, offered my sympathies and my prayers, and saw him off. And I felt very chastened and very humbled. How silly of me to burst in with my stupid story without first ascertaining his mood! That was a violent imposition, an insensitive outburst, a mechanical behavior. I had been speaking to my friend of yesterday, not to my friend of today; to my memory of him, not to the reality I had in front of me; to a shadow, not to a person. I had taken him for granted with the dangerous familiarity of our daily contact. I had assumed that his day today would be like any other day, and all assumptions are great deceivers. I had fallen into the trap of guiding my present by my past.

If only I had looked into his face! That was the first thing I should have done, my first act of friendship, my recognition of him as a person. To look into his eyes. There was sorrow all over them. They spoke his anxiety and his pain. When I allowed him to speak, his first words were, "My son." If I had looked into his eyes I would have found the word written there. The face is always new. The eyes are always alive. They speak, they tell, they warn. But to understand their language one has to have the sense to look at them. And I had been blind at the moment. I had lost touch with my friend. A few hours in between had been enough to create a gap, because much had happened in that time. To keep pace with the other person I have always to follow my own movements and to follow his. To watch the lines of his face and the light of his eyes. To start every time anew, treasuring past memories, but only as the fertile ground for the present experience.

There is a phrase that embodies a whole program of life: "Every time we meet is the first time." There is a thrill and a pulse in that sentence. Imagine that a friend tells me, "Remember the first time we met?" And imagine that I am able to answer in spontaneity and truth, "Every time we meet is the first time." I know of no higher ideal of human relationship. We have known each other for years, we have met hundreds of times, we can recite each other's life by heart . . . and yet, in full truth and ready experience, this meeting is new, this encounter is original, this time is the first time we meet. Tell me your name. Open your soul. Let me look in wonder and love at that miracle which is you, and which I know so well and at the same time I am only beginning to know. Philosophers say that the individual is "ineffable," and, without the terminology, that is what I experience in direct impact. I know you so well that, precisely *because* of that, I know there is much more to you that I do not know yet, and I want to discover it day by day—appearing before you with the conceptual innocence of a first meeting, without prejudices, without stereotypes, without memories, to see the light on your face as if for the first time and to listen to the music of your voice as to an unpublished symphony in private premiere.

Every time we meet is the first time, because every time you are different, as I also am. We do not step twice in the same river, said Heraclitus; this was said very truly, as the river flows without end and its waters are never the same. How much more so when it is not water but mood and temper and heart and soul and breath and life. We do not enter twice in the same life, the life of a friend, because life flows and runs and sings like the waters of the river of paradise over the fields of creation. By the time I catch up with you, you are miles ahead in the lively hide-and-seek of our meetings and our partings. Now I understand why I feel so thrilled when I come to see you: I sense in my heart of hearts that you will be different, new, reborn, and I long to see your new face and to hear your new voice. I love you, my friend, and I come to you with the novel openness of my tender admiration for your ever new presence before my marveled eyes. Let our meetings be ever new, that our friendship be ever alive.

28

Social Masks

Good manners are the spice of social life. They make eyes meet, hands touch, and human beings pay attention to each other in the whirl of a hurried existence, be it even for a fleeting moment of recognition and friendliness while the rest of mankind ignore each other with cold indifference. A polite word with the right intonation at the right time can help smooth out the rough edges of daily coexistence in an unfriendly world. It must have been a kind soul who invented those chosen words of gracious courtesy that ennoble language and frame all of life's circumstances, from a chance encounter to a condolence visit. The well-bred person fits in smoothly wherever he is and whatever he says.

But then there is that other side of the social world, the one of formal etiquette and rigid manners. The artificiality, the stiffness, the emptiness. The opposite of spontaneity—no warmth, no sincerity, no real contact. And the more the empty rituals of social behavior encroach into our own language, gestures, and attitudes, the more we lose our own personality and individuality. The mask of social etiquette can obliterate the features of a human face.

How are you today? Fine, thank you. And what about you? Pulling along. That is what we all are doing. Pulling along somehow or other, and we do not stop to give others detailed information on how we are getting along, just as we do not expect nor want it from them. It would be a little awkward if, when we ask an acquaintance we happen to meet on the road, "How are you doing?" he would begin to tell us right there, standing in the middle of the street: "Well, since you ask me, this is how things are with me just now, more or less. This morning I'm not feeling well, my stomach is acting up and I'm feeling giddy; I've taken some medicine, but if I don't get better I'll go to the doctor this evening. Then I'm all worked up because my wife's parents want to join us for the holidays, and I don't know how I'll manage to keep them off, and even less how I'll manage if they come with us. Besides, I've asked for a loan to buy my car, and it's turning out to be much more burdensome than I had anticipated. On top of that. . . ." By then our friend will most likely find himself talking alone in the middle of the street, while we have swiftly disappeared around the nearest corner. It is true that we had asked him how he was doing, but everybody understands that the phrase does not mean what it says but exactly the opposite. We use it precisely when we do not want the other person to tell us how he is doing. We talk without talking. We meet without meeting. Today I saw so-and-so. How is he doing? Fine. That is, I do not have the slightest idea, because we only exchanged platitudes. We live without living. He is not he, and I am not I. We make a show of contact that precludes all contact. That is the way we lose our beings in the labyrinth of daily living.

The English language has carried to its ultimate perfection the ritual of mutual introduction. To the first venture, "How do you do?" the official answer is the exact mirror image, "How do you do?" Two questions and no answer. That is, questions that are no questions in a meeting that is no meeting between persons who at that moment are no persons. In fact, if the introduction is merely a formal one in a group of several persons, maybe no more words are exchanged between the two new mutually acquainted people.

Citizens of a certain beleaguered country, when asked how they fare in their country, are in the habit of answering, "Very fine; . . . or, shall I tell?" And with that they stop at the "very fine." The rubric has done its duty. Some people also, when they shake hands—particularly if there are several people around—shake hands with one person while looking or even speaking with another. A bodily lie. My hand is with one, and my eyes with another. Ritual adultery. My body should be all of a piece wherever it is and with whomsoever it is. And my body should express what is in my mind, or again I am split inside myself, and my existence is not whole. Polite expressions often cheat us of truth and prevent us from being our true selves.

In a condolence meeting I attended at the death of a public person, seventeen short speeches were made about the deceased. After some time I realized that none of the speakers was saying anything at all except trite platitudes on the general occasion of a person's death. I reflected that if the name of the deceased were left out of the speeches, they would be perfectly well suited to a similar occasion with another name. His death has been a great loss. Nobody could imagine such a sudden end. His contribution was unique. His place will never quite be filled. I always had the highest respect for him and for his work. We understand the grief of his family and pray for strength for them in this moment of trial. They may rest assured that their beloved elder will have a fitting reward in heaven. May God rest his soul. Amen. How do you do? How do you do? And I am left with no idea whatever of what those seventeen people thought of the dead man. Wasn't there among them a close friend who could have broken the wall of officialism with a glimpse of personal intimacy?

A humourous Indian writer describes the outward goings and the inward feelings of a social party among well-behaved people. Give us a song! they ask one man. Yes, yes, he is shy but we know his art! Come on, don't let us down! The man graciously obliges to everybody's consternation, and when he finishes all cheer enthusiastically and someone feels obliged to ask for an encore. Give us another one! And he does. There is no way of stopping him, song after song with merciless cheer. When the food arrives, it is so pungent that it can hardly be kept in the mouth, and all ask for water to relieve the burning sensation. Yet all praise the food before the smiling hostess who shyly confesses to having prepared it herself. Then comes the turn to tell jokes, and to suffer at hearing the same stories told in the same way and having to laugh at the end. The hostess leads a conducted tour of the house to show the improvements she has brought about to be admired sheepishly by all. What a delightful time we had! Such a perfect party! We'll soon be inviting you to our party. From today on, the guests start planning their vengeance with their own parties. Social life has to go on.

In an international music festival I was listening to a world-famous orchestra under a world-famous conductor in the inspired performance of a classical program. In the middle of the program, however, between a divertimento by Mozart and a symphony by Mahler, which were superbly interpreted by the orchestra and warmly appreciated by the enthusiastic audience, the conductor had introduced a short piece of modern atonal music whose author I will not even mention. This piece was made up of a few stray sounds in random succession without melody, harmony, rhythm, or art of any recognizable kind, played with resignation and conducted with indifference. When the sounds ceased as aimlessly as they had begun there was a moment of silence in the hall. None of those loud, spontaneous, politely boisterous upheavals that followed Mozart and Mahler. The well-dressed and highly sensitive ladies and gentlemen in the audience hesitated for a moment about what to do. I observed them looking at each other with amused looks on their faces and a slight shrugging of their shoulders, till at last shyly, politely, minimally, reluctantly they clapped as well-bred audiences are supposed to clap after worthy performances. I did not clap. I would not shout my protest, but I did signal it by not clapping when I did not feel like it. And if all those worthy people in the audience, who had not at all enjoyed the atonal bit, had also kept a respectful silence, and would do the same whenever a similar outrage is committed in any such musical program, that would bring an end to the abuse of interspersing doubtful music in a classical program. Let there by all means be concerts of atonal music where their patrons can enjoy it and clap their hands numb in applause. But do not let a classical performance be defaced by unworthy antiques. This abuse exists and thrives because people are too polite and follow the etiquette of the applause when they should rather show the truth of their genuine disapproval. Artificial approval does not help the arts.

The mask of politeness can freeze the features of liveliness on the human face. The mask can be comfortable and can help avoid embarrassment, but the mask is not my face, and so I ultimately want to discard it. In the following personal incident I experienced the pain and the relief of removing the mask at an awkward moment.

I was staying with an Indian family and shared their daily meals with them in happy company. The woman in the house took care that the meals would be varied and tasty, and watched in my face my reactions to her cooking. Since she was an excellent cook I could afford to let myself go and allow my face to show my delight at her delicacies. One day, however, there was trouble. A favorite dish of Gujarati cuisine is a pasta-like flour cake served with a pungent sauce. When that dish is prepared, it takes up the whole meal, and nothing else is served that day. I have a fairly universal taste, and there are few preparations I cannot stomach, but this is one of them. That set the stage for the showdown. I sat cross-legged on the floor of the kitchen with the large metal dish in front of me, looked up for the menu, and saw the housewife with the obnoxious preparation in her hands, ready to serve me with a large smile and a joyful announcement: "See what I have prepared today for you. You like it, don't you?" A nice plight I was in. If she had mentioned her culinary plans earlier in the day and asked my opinion, I could have expressed my reservations, and the menu could have been changed in time. Again, if there was something else to eat, I could decline what was not to my taste and make up for it with the rest. But I knew there was only one dish, I genuinely disliked it, and I was being asked about it at the moment of being served. What was I to say?

My first impulse was to lie plainly and say: "Who does not like it? Such a good dish! I have eaten it a number of times, and I will fully enjoy it. Give me a full helping!" I have told such lies many times in my life, and one more would not make any difference, and would certainly get me out of the quandary. Many times I have eaten dishes I do not relish, and nothing would happen if I did it once more. So I was quite ready to put on the mask and eat and praise the food. But then I woke up. I knew the woman, I trusted her friendship, I fancied the adventure; and so, looking up at her with tenderness in my voice and sincerity on my face, I said, "I wish I could tell you I like this, and I certainly appreciate your special care for me in thinking out today's menu, but since you ask me—and with the sincerity your very affection inspires in me—I have to say that I do not like this dish. I can eat it willingly, but it is definitely not to my taste."

The scene that followed can be imagined. The protestations, the regrets, the proposal to get food from the neighbors, my refusal to have her do any such thing, her resolution never again to take anything for granted, my pain at having spoken but my satisfaction that I would not be made to eat something distasteful to me, the makeshift sandwich I ate, and the clouded enjoyment of the favorite dish by everybody else. But then a large crop of positive results followed the stormy meal. For one thing, our relationship grew in intimacy and confidence as I had dared to speak the truth and they had taken it sportingly. Then my credibility also grew, and in the future when I praised a dish they knew I meant it, because they knew that I had the courage to speak my mind frankly. By saying that I did not like one dish I had aquired the right to be believed when I said I liked others; and this credibility extended itself naturally from the kitchen to life itself so that my word has been more weighty and reliable since that day. And one final advantage: When I go to that house for a meal I know I will not be given that dish again! The courage to drop all masks and be oneself, always pays in the end.

29

How Not to Enjoy a Film

I know two ways of ruining the viewing of a good film, the reading of a good book, the watching of a good play. One is to come to it with very high expectations of what it is going to be, realize then that it is not so great after all, and thus say resignedly at the end, Yes, it was good . . . but I thought it was going to be better. The other way is to come without prejudice but to find early in the proceedings a similarity to another film, book, or play; to make a mental comparison between the old and the new, and again say at the end with a tone of tired wisdom, Yes, it was good . . . but the other was better. Comparison and expectation. Past and future. A sure way to ruin the present.

Each thing is valid in itself. Every face has its beauty and every word its music. But we have a huge repository of thick files in our memory, and no sooner has a concept entered our minds or a sensation our senses, than we rummage through our files, find a precedent, set the new experience against the old, and proclaim with unfailing judgment that the old one was better. We know. We have experienced better times and higher standards. Tastes are deteriorating and talents are drifting. That earlier performance was the real thing, the genuine article, the unsurpassed climax. All the rest reflect lower standards and lesser minds. We indulgently listen and watch, but inside ourselves we know we are witnesses to a minor show—we, who had been privileged to attend the star spectacle. The comparison with the best lessens the enjoyment of the good.

The great Indian thinker and writer Kalelkar used to say that he enjoyed Indian classical music precisely because he did not understand much about it. He quoted a friend of his who knew too much, had listened to the greatest maestros in their best moments, and inevitably referred to them in his mind when listening to other musicians. This made it impossible for him to enjoy any such performance, however good it might be in itself. He grew impatient, displeased, unsatisfied. He had tasted the best, and could never again be satisfied with the second best. The very phrase "second best" is a condemnation although it purports to be a commendation. The word "best" is in it, but by making it "second" it pushes the described object back under the shadows of rejection. I guess the people who least enjoy a concert are the music critics who have to write a review afterward. Too much knowledge may blunt the capacity for innocent enjoyment.

I once watched a movie with a friend who has the blissful capacity of enjoying everything as though it were the only thing to be enjoyed and the first time he enjoyed it. He has the blessing of a child's eyes and a child's capacity for utmost wonder and instant joy. More than watching the movie I enjoyed watching him watch the movie. In fact the movie was one of those follow-ups to a successful first film, made to cash in on the popularity of the first one by offering a sequel with the same name, the same actors, and almost the same plot. I had seen the first part, and so I was secretly comparing in my mind the second with the first, and deciding that the first had been really good whereas the second was a poor replay with repetitious sequences and a predictable end. I said so to my friend during the intermission, and added the obvious explanation of why he was enjoying the picture while I was not: "You have not seen the first part, of course, and so you find this one enjoyable; but for me this is only a mediocre repetition and I am bored." To my surprise he answered, "I too saw the first part when it came out and enjoyed it. But this also is fine! Forget about the other and get into this one, and you'll see how you enjoy this one too." There was such an obvious genuineness in his voice, such joy in his face and such truth in his emphasis that his sincerity touched me and I went back into the theater after the intermission with a new spirit and a fresh eye. And I enjoyed the movie. My friend was right. I had let the first part weigh over the second, I had let the comparison rule my mind and ruin my capacity to look afresh and appreciate something for its own sake.

I know a woman who is unhappy with her husband, splendid man though he is, because her sister married a better man, and the shadow of a brighter match has darkened her own. She has no complaint against her husband and there is nothing wrong with her marriage as such . . . except that her sister's marriage was more glamorous and this made her feel inferior and underrate her own husband. And I know more than a few students who respond with little enthusiasm when I congratulate them on a very high result in an important examination . . . because, though their result is undoubtedly high, their classroom rival has obtained an even higher one, and that spoils the feast. Now, since in almost every activity of life and for almost every one of us there is always someone higher and cleverer and luckier, we have here a sure way to make ourselves miserable whatever happens in whatever circumstances. Just look around, see who has scored higher or done better or come out ahead, and grieve and sulk accordingly for the rest of the season . . . till the next test comes and you repeat the performance, the search, and the mourning in fateful succession. It is time we stop looking at others and ruling our lives by the shadows that others cast on our own.

An even more insidious trap is our naive readiness to let others rule our lives with their judgments of us. People are prompt to judge and to express opinions of other people, and we are only too prone to be impressed by their strictures and depressed by their condemnations. If I do not allow comparison with others to lower my self-esteem, much less can I allow comparison or judgment by others to rule in any way my mood and my worth. I am not speaking here of healthy criticism and friendly feedback which are welcome and necessary aids to self-analysis and genuine progress; I am referring to the nagging, adverse, discouraging remarks of people who presume to put me down on their own authority. They are surely free to tell me what they want but I too am free to react with firm humility and genuine freedom to keep my distance and steady my life.

I find that the best answer to such frontal attacks is an equally frontal reaction, which usually stops the critic in his or her tracks and settles the question. A concrete example: Someone tells me, "You are selfish." Instead of countering with a defense or a negative I grant his point and answer, "In your opinion." And before he has had time to react, I add in the same peaceful tone: "Which I respect and do not share." Quite often this plain statement is enough to parry the blow and discourage any further attack. Sometimes, however, the critic insists, "It is not only my opinion; everybody thinks the same." Then a simple question suffices: "How do you know?" It is not easy to know how the whole world thinks about a particular point or person, and in any case there is always a remark to be added: "I also form part of the whole world and my opinion is different. That, for me, is the main opinion." The point is not to argue about the point itself— "You are selfish," "No, I am not selfish," "Yes, you are"—which is a blow-for-a-blow without solution and without end, for the more I deny the more he asserts with no possible meeting point. On the contrary, I grant his point for a start, and I accept it; I take notice that he believes me to be selfish, and recognize his right to believe it. I do not quarrel with that, and therefore not with him. At the same time I bring politely to his attention the point that his opinion might not be universal and in any case differs from mine. I do not argue. I do not attempt to prove that he is wrong and his opinion unfounded. I do not get involved in a totally fruitless discussion; I acknowledge his position and assert mine. I keep my distance and save his dignity. I even show appreciation of the fact that he has volunteered information about how he sees me, which is something I am interested in knowing as part of my total awareness, without being swayed or disturbed by this unfavorable opinion of me. This simple way of reacting has brought me peace more than once. The advice comes from Carl Rogers: "My locus of evaluation is inside myself." No comparison with others, no outside judgment is to be allowed to rule my life. I take it all in, and I decide the outcome. That, in any case, is my opinion.

30

The Happiness Trap

A friend once taught me the importance in our lives of hidden assumptions. We often disagree, quarrel, are confused and suffer deeply without solution because we tackle our problems at their apparent level where the tangle cannot be unraveled, and forget their hidden roots which alone can give a key to the proper handling of the situation. To uncover hidden assumptions is a healthy and profitable occupation that can clear up much unnecessary suffering and misunderstanding.

One of the basic assumptions in life, maybe the first and deepest one, is that we are supposed to be happy. And I am beginning to think, humbly and tentatively, that the assumption may not be true after all—and what an immense relief it would be if we were to put it aside! The pursuit of happiness, the need to be and feel and appear happy, the sense of guilt and frustration when in spite of all efforts we do not achieve a happy feeling, the burden of attaining the unattainable—all of that would suddenly disappear; we could then relax in quiet acquiescence, almost happy at the thought of not having to strive anymore to be happy. Maybe we are spoiling our happiness by trying too hard to be happy.

This is perhaps the heaviest conditioning we have submitted to in our lives, and the one with the most grievous consequences. In particular, religious people like myself feel themselves doubly under the commandment "Thou shalt be happy," as they represent God before humanity and thus feel they would be letting God down if they should appear sad and downcast; this would imply that the service of God is a dismal job instead of the glorious privilege it has to be by its very definition, *Servire Deo est regnare:* To serve God is to be a king. We want to be happy in order to show that God's grace works, that the Kingdom is already in our hearts, that there is hope for the world; and particularly we want to be and appear happy in order to make our way of life appealing to young people and so to attract vocations that will continue our work and give us a sense of security and satisfaction. We believe that our own happiness will enable people to see in us a source of joy and a reason to hope in the midst of a world full of suffering. These are all very good reasons for us to strive after genuine happiness.

And yet we do not find the commandment an easy one. In a recent meeting with a number of religious men and women, a devout Sister stood up and asked me point-blank, "Why are religious people not happy?" I respected for a moment the heavy silence her question caused in the hall, and then I said with as much gentleness as I could muster, "Sister, are you saying that you are not happy?" She broke down and cried. She had only projected onto others her own dissatisfaction, but the faces in the hall told me visibly that the question was not an idle one. Happiness does not come easily even to people who profess to have freed themselves from the worries of life and to anticipate on earth a glimpse of the heavenly city.

In a certain Latin American country I was invited to participate in a religious TV program with the ambitious title, "Time to Be Happy." The genial showman began asking the crowd, "What time is it?" and they all answered loudly, "Time to be happy!" (In fact the man was so popular that people recognized him in the streets and asked him whenever they saw him, "What time is it?" and then it was his turn to answer with a smile,

"Time to be happy!") Then the program went on. He asked, "Let all those who are happy in this gathering lift up their hands." And everybody in the crowd obediently lifted their hands without any exception. It was nice to watch the picture on the TV monitor. The trouble was that I was present in the hall, and had seen the audience rehearse the answer to the question and the lifting of the hands. At the beginning the crowd had been distracted and unresponsive, and had to be urged, exhorted, prodded into a loud, massive, and seemingly spontaneous answer. "What time is it? Come on, louder and *all* of you. What time is it? Once again. Shout more. And now all hands up. All at the same time and all straight and high. Are you not happy? Everybody here has to be happy. Come on, one, two, three, all hands up!" And so it went on for quite a time. Rehearsed happiness. Practiced show. Artificial response.

It was pitiful to see the people trying to appear happy, lifting their hands, waving them in unison, now to the right, now to the left, all properly done till everything came out perfect. Only after about half an hour of practice was the response found satisfactory, and so the filming began. It showed beautifully on the screen. And it felt all miserable from the inside. To make matters worse, after a while there was a break in the filming. Something had gone wrong, and we had to start all over again: "What time is it?" "Time to be happy!" All hands up and all smiles on. I suffered through the show. And then even its very name hurt me. People had to find a special time to be happy, one hour a week on Channel 6, to make up somehow for the rest of the week. On the whole not a very happy experience.

In another South American country, Argentina, I experienced the thrill of reading at a stretch José Hernández' epic poem *Martín Fierro* and identifying for a while with the *gaucho* in its verses —the frontiersman, neither Spaniard nor Indian, who with his horse and his knife as his only possessions rides the pampas in proud solitude, friend to stars and birds, ready to kill and to die, perennial singer of man's destiny on a desolate earth. The last verses of the long poem sum up his extensive pilgrimage through land, men, and ideas, and he says poignantly that all he has narrated is only

> evils known to all of old,
> but which no one ever told.

His autobiography can be summed up with a single word: "evils." That is what he has set down in his poem, because that has been his whole life. And the point is that those evils are known to all, but all have keep quiet about them, and all try to deceive themselves and life itself by making it appear better than what it is in guilty conspiracy. "But which no one ever told." This last line is sheer anger and spite against all those who keep quiet about life's miseries, thinking that by glossing over them they can suppress them or at least forget them. All the courage and sincerity and faith of the gaucho are needed to tell the truth of life in the face of a dissembling and distracted society. And it is only then that poetry is born in the midst of truth, and life can be sung in all its misery and all its beauty. It is by being close to nature that we can understand its message, and by accepting solitude that we can reach the hearts of many. Let us not hide the evils of life if we want to reach its reality.

Once I was visiting a religious fair lavishly organized by an active sect of a certain religion. Its devotees were at hand to guide the visitor, explain every display, hand out propaganda leaflets, and, above all, smile unceasingly with a blissful countenance that spoke more than any picture or argument of the happiness that was theirs in the pursuit of their beliefs and that could come to anyone who would join their faith. All went smoothly for me till, somewhat mischievously, I went behind a partition that separated from the public a private area meant only for the followers of the sect. There were no smiles there. The same people who glowed with happiness before the outside visitors, were here tense and tired, talking harshly to each other, and even throwing things around with obvious temper. One of them noticed my presence, came to meet me while drawing everybody's attention to me in the process, and all of a sudden the whole atmosphere changed. The smiles flashed again. They were switched on as if by regular practice. I was sweetly asked what I wanted; I asked my way to the main stand, was very kindly escorted to it, and the curtain closed behind me to let them brood and quarrel at ease. I had seen the fair.

Serious and honest thinkers have not hesitated to express the hard truth about human life. Bertrand Russell writes in his autobiography: "I am amazed at the number of people who are wretched almost beyond endurance." And, "The world seems to me quite dreadful; the unhappiness of most people is very great, and I often wonder how they all endure it."* Thoreau has also said that "most men live lives of quiet desperation." Schweitzer said of himself that he had known very few happy moments in his life. A great Indian, and leader of the Jain community in Bombay, once wrote in the paper of which he was the editor an autobiographical article with the title "I am an unhappy man," in which, without any self-pity, cynicism, or morbid exhibitionism, he plainly and objectively stated the heavy trials and dull routine of an otherwise rich, honest, fruitful, and honored life. These ponderous testimonies weigh heavily against the facile optimism that sees happiness everywhere, but which brings ultimately a greater frustration, as sometimes it seems to be nowhere.

A fervent priest tells me in a letter just received: "I am determined to make this year a year of deep permanent happiness for me to mark the silver jubilee of my priesthood." A beautiful thought which I respect and admire in my brother priest; but, to my mind and understanding, a dangerous trap that may convert

* Bertrand Russell, *Autobiography*, Allen & Unwin, 1975, pp. 179, 194.

his jubilee into something quite different from what he expects. He is not likely to achieve twelve months of deep permanent happiness, and at the end he will be faced with a painful dilemma. He may be honest and sensitive enough to see and admit that his resolve has not worked, and that straight realization would cast a shadow over his enthusiasm for even the best cause on earth. If even one's exalted state at its mature best does not yield reliable happiness, what else will? Or he may blind himself to the facts, push away from his awareness the bitter disappointment, and declare to the world and to himself that it has been indeed a magnificent year full of blessings from the Lord and satisfaction from humanity in measure far beyond all his expectations. The best of people do such things; they innocently practice self-deception in the belief that they have only undergone a trial of faith to give them greater happiness later, and that they are bound to uphold God's image as the unfailing dispenser of happiness for his own credit and for the good of mankind. Or there is a third possibility—that good priest may simply and conveniently forget his resolution and its failure, and go on till his golden jubilee twenty-five years later, which by then he may celebrate in a more sober manner.

Happiness is not obtained by a resolution to obtain it; and, going deeper, happiness need not be associated with so called happy occasions or holy memories, however legitimate these may be. This is the underlying assumption I am uncovering here. Prize your priesthood, thank the Lord for it, mark this year with the generous renewal of your consecration to God and his people, but do not program joy and happiness by appointment, because that is not the way life works.

In contrast, I heard a public figure say candidly, almost charmingly, in an interview: "I am not happy, and why should I be?" The spontaneity with which she pronounced those challenging words took away the contemptible tone they could otherwise have had. She had done away with the assumption that we all are supposed to be happy, and such a matter-of-fact attitude to life as it is, and as we usually do not like it to be, lent credibility and wholeness to her views and her personality. Nowhere is it written that I must be happy, she implied with those words, and so I live my life as it comes with its ups and downs, not measuring moods or comparing degrees or striving for records. There is sanity and balance in that approach.

A schoolboy asked Krishnamurti after a talk in his school, "Sir, are you happy?" It is interesting, to begin with, that it was a schoolboy who asked the question. In the many talks Krishnamurti gave in his lifetime and the hundreds of questions that were recorded from different audiences in different countries, only a child, so far as I know, dared to ask the direct question. Others asked philosophical questions, personal questions, practical questions, theoretical questions—but no adult, no inquirer, no seeker had the courage and the simplicity of asking the most intimate and most threatening question a person can be asked: Are you happy? I say threatening because nobody wants to admit that he or she is unhappy, due precisely to the universal conditioning which makes happiness the goal of life and sentences to shame those who do not achieve it. So one could answer, Of course I am happy, I am a happy person, there are ups and downs in my life as in everybody else's but all in all I consider myself a happy man, I cannot complain, I've had my trials but I'm reasonably happy, you can see for yourself that I look happy and prosperous, don't I? Or one could give a roundabout answer by going into the definition of happiness, its true meaning of deep peace compatible with troubled moods, its ultimate foundation on faith in life and in God whatever may happen in any pleasant or unpleasant occasion of life. The question is in any case difficult because few people are personally aware of their level of happiness, and fewer are ready to disclose it before a chance questioner.

Krishnamurti was a man supremely in touch with himself and

disarmingly honest in his answers. It is true that his answers were often directed not to the superficial question but to its deeper background and its hidden presuppositions; for rather than providing clear-cut answers he sought to make the inquirer think and find the final answer by him- or herself. But in this case the questioner was a schoolboy and the atmosphere simple and intimate, and that made Krishnamurti's answer all the more valuable and definitive. The boy asked, "Sir, are you happy?" and Krishnamurti answered at once, "I don't know. I haven't thought about it. But if I begin to think about it I'll definitely feel unhappy."

Blessed be the person who has not stopped to think whether he is happy or unhappy, and to whom the question has not even occurred. Blessed will he be if he is free from the need to be happy, to appear happy, to have to answer to the direct question that of course he is happy indeed, and that if he were to be given his life over again he would choose the same course and tread the same path, as this one has given him true happiness. Blessed is he if he can simply and truly say, I don't know. That question is not on my conscience, that problem is not in my life. I am free from the conditioning that makes man's life on earth revolve around the obsession of his personal happiness. And I don't want to think about it, so as not to fall into the trap that would definitely make me unhappy.

Happiness is like health. The moment you start talking about it, there is something wrong with it. The healthy man does not think about his health, does not talk about it, does not go about asking people, Are you healthy? Whoever does that shows that he is not healthy himself. A healthy body lives its health without being conscious of it. A happy person lives his happiness without thinking about it. The day he worries about it, he has lost it. Happiness is like a shoe: If one forgets one is wearing it, it fits. But if one begins to check whether it hurts or not, that is a bad sign. Happiness is like a game, like a sport. If you stop in the midst of a game of tennis or of cards to think whether you are enjoying it . . . you are not!

All the thinking, striving, preaching, writing, teaching, exhorting people to be happy is a noble exercise that in the end defeats its purpose. The theory of happiness may be best left alone. The best effect of this chapter will be to be able to forget it after having read it. A truly happy ending.

31

The Bamboo Leaf

This is a story told of the Buddha. He was once sitting down in the presence of his disciples when a fly alighted on his forehead. He immediately waved it away with a quick movement of his hand. The fly flew away. Then, in the silence that ensued, the Buddha slowly, deliberately repeated the same movement and brought his hand to his forehead though the fly was not there anymore. The disciples noticed the puzzling behavior of their master, and one of them had the courage to ask him the straight question: "You are waving away a fly from your forehead when there is no fly. Can you tell us the meaning of your action?" The master explained: "When the fly landed on my skin I instinctively reacted and drove it away with a reflex movement. I was actually not conscious of what I was doing. The action literally escaped me and was not under my consciousness. I want to be aware of all that I do, and that is why I now have repeated the gesture as my own gesture. My body is my body, and so my gestures have to be my gestures."

An important facet of being myself is being my body, which is a very close, intimate, familiar . . . and yet very unfamiliar part of me. My own undiscovered backyard. My neglected half. My ignored self. Not that I have to control each movement like a machine or behave like an automaton. On the contrary. I have to be supple and gentle and spontaneous in my body as in my mind. The point is that just as my thoughts are mine, so must also my gestures be truly mine, and my heart and soul be in them as they are in my thoughts and in my emotions. I have written in one of the initial chapters about the conditioning of the body, the muscles and nerves and joints and bones. I want to regain now, as I go on rediscovering and reowning myself, my friendship with my body for the healthy integration of my whole being. To be aware of what I do not only with my mind and my heart, but also with my hands and my feet. They also are part of me.

Mr. and Mrs. Eugene Herrigel went to Japan to study Zen. The husband did it through the study of archery, while the wife through the pursuit of flower arrangement. The method is immaterial, the spirit and the training are what counts, and both people left signal testimony of their experience in two parallel books that provide delightful reading and profound teaching. It is of the greatest interest to watch a purposeful German philosopher take up bow and arrow, strain every nerve and try purposefully to hit the bull's-eye under the silent critical look of the master who teasingly discourages every effort and discounts every hit. It was a six-year endeavor. The more the German strove with calculated precision to achieve perfection (he was already an expert rifleman), the more the Japanese teacher found fault with his effort, his tension, his preoccupation with hitting the mark. The body has to be one with the mind, and follow almost by itself the unexpressed thought as the hands follow the eye, and the eye of the body follows the eye of the mind in the organic unity of the whole integrated human being. When the body is taken into confidence it does not any more "obey" the mind, but cooperates with it on its own, aware of the plans and eager to contribute its part in them. Easy to say and hard to do.

The breathing is perfected till it regulates with its deep, vital, personal rhythm all that the mind and body do in friendly unison; the hands find their position, holding the bow effortlessly and drawing the string as it is asking to be drawn, while the arms and shoulders remain relaxed and the whole body enjoys a unified, common peace till the right moment is reached and the arrow "shoots itself" and flies where it knows it has to fly, straight to the target that is inviting its visit and gently drawing it into itself. All this sounds like a piece of poetry to Western ears, but was businesslike instruction coming from the Japanese teacher. One can easily imagine the German professor's frustration throughout the six years of painful learning.

The master teaches that in order to achieve a perfect shot with the arrow one has to stop thinking about the shot, waiting in patience for the action to happen by itself, forgetting oneself and one's aims and calculations. As Eugene Herrigel wrote in *Zen in the Art of Archery*, "You haven't really let go of yourself. It is all so simple. You can learn from an ordinary bamboo leaf what ought to happen. It bends lower and lower under the weight of the snow. Suddenly the snow slips to the ground without the leaf having stirred. Stay like that at the point of highest tension until the shot falls from you. So, indeed, it is: when the tension is fulfilled, the shot *must* fall, it must fall from the archer like snow from a bamboo leaf, before he even thinks it."*

The body is no longer an instrument but a partner. The enhanced awareness of the senses is in communion with the mind, enabling it to know the right time for the right thing to happen and letting it happen with nature's ease as the bent bamboo leaf releases the piled-up snow and snaps back resiliently into its own gracious curve. Behind the beautiful imagery of language there is the pain of the long effort required to recover the lost contact with our own bodies. We suffer under the estrangement caused by a moralistic suspicion against the body as an agent of evil, to be submitted by the soul into bonded silence through stern discipline and rigorous privations. Man's evil tendency is actually

---

* Eugene Herrigel, *Zen in the Art of Archery*, Vintage Books, 1971, p. 54.

in the mind, but this mind, in a treacherous plot, has accused the senses of being the agents of evil and declared a holy war on them to divert attention from its own wrongdoings. It is time we establish justice and make the mind silent while the body recovers its healthy balance and its natural wisdom, so that it can choose instinctively what is good for it and therefore for the whole of the being to which it intrinsically belongs.

The East has developed more the bodily aspect of our lives, and its books, both ancient and modern, are full of stories that illustrate the role of a friendly body in an integrated life. Gichin Funakoshi tells one such story about one of the great karate masters of his time, Isoku. He was the noblest leader in the region, but a young teacher who thought much of himself calculated that he could defeat Isoku if he caught him unawares. To that purpose he spied his way through the city at night, approached him silently from behind, and delivered a crushing blow to overturn him. Isoku was so alert and self-possessed in body and mind that he caught the blow in his stride without swerving an inch, and at the same instant with lightning speed, without even so much as turning to see who his attacker was or to locate him visually, he flashed his right hand behind himself without altering in the least his walking pace, caught in a steel grip the hand of the bewildered assailant and dragged him along like a helpless burden without deigning to so much as look at him. The trapped youngster, humbled and hurt in the viselike squeeze, finally asked for pardon, and only then did Isoku speak. He asked matter-of-factly, "And who are you?" He said his name. Isoku commented gently, "You should not play such tricks with an old man like me." Then he let go of his grip, and continued his walk at the same pace as though nothing had happened.

Such composure, alertness, strength, peace, and humor reveal the total development of a human being in all aspects. This has much to teach those people who are trained in an excessively

intellectual atmosphere to the detriment of their other potentialities. Each one is heir to his or her own tradition, and that is to
be accepted with gratitude and generosity; but now that people
travel and cultures mix and books are translated and curiosity
increases and one half of mankind comes to know not only how
the other half lives, but also how it thinks and reasons and acts,
we all can and should enrich our past experience with new approaches.

It is, to me, amazingly true how bodily peace helps one to gain
and establish mental peace. A tense body makes for a tense
mind, and an intimately relaxed body infallibly harbors a relaxed
mind. We who strive so much after peace of mind could profit by
learning the ways of peace in the body. There are schools and
techniques, books and practices of all kinds, and many can be
useful if properly undertaken, but the important thing is the
personal interest, the inner realization, the genuine desire to
enter into communion with the body and value it and trust it.
Then it will relax by itself, and its own well-being will prepare
and foster and maintain the well-being of the soul it loves. Let
the bamboo leaf feel by itself the weight of the snow that keeps
falling on it throughout the winter of life, let it know its fiber
and choose its time, let it shake the burden at the right instant
when it is asking to be dropped, and spring back to freshness in
the spontaneity of nature's own play.

One day, during Eugene Herrigel's strenuous lessons, after
years of sweat and frustration and resistance, after a shot whose
perfection he himself had not realized, the persevering pupil saw
his teacher turn to him and take a deep bow in silence. He knew
he had made it. The arrow had shot itself. And his life had been
changed.

At about the same time, and after about the same strain and
the same despair, his wife also attained to the effortless grace of
letting the flowers arrange themselves through her trained and

now supple fingers. Their experiences had changed their lives forever. It had taken six years.

The importance of this teaching follows from the forgotten principle: Awareness of the body is our best practical and personal link with the present moment.

32

The Playful Child

Together with the body and the senses, a feature that is asking with loud insistence to be developed is the child we all carry within us. The playful child. The mischievous, romping, unpredictable child. The source of joy, creativity, and spontaneity that brings liveliness to our work and love to our hearts. The role of the child in us is the same as the role of the child in a family: Amidst the daily troubles and nagging frictions, unending problems and severe trials, the presence of a child in the home is light and warmth, is life and energy, is the reminder to forget suffering and remember we were once children and can continue to be so to our advantage, bringing to our adulthood the endearing qualities of the playful child.

The child is not dead in us. It is only smothered under the layers of training, scolding, teaching, threatening, coaxing, and seducing that make up a child's education in a respectable family. We have lost our smile and hidden our mischief in the lowest recesses of our personality, afraid of being called childish in a world of adults. No, we are serious, we are mature, we are responsible and can hold for hours without blinking a conversation in which we have no interest whatsoever, smiling and nodding all the while as though we were deeply interested indeed. That art, if art it is, we have mastered to the dulling of our senses and the deadening of our lives. If we manage to awaken the child in us and give him a place in our grown-up life, we shall find a new freshness and liveliness in our heart, and shall be able to communicate it to all those around us, which will be the best contribution we can make to the welfare of society. Today's world especially needs a child's laughter to survive. And again the important point: The child is charmingly alive because he or she is a creature of the present moment.

A child has fantasy, creativity, originality, can see wonders in a pebble and fairies in a wood. The child can create a private dream world in the dullest of circumstances and enjoy the creation with full zest. Once I watched two children play on a dusty road. They had arranged a few stones in some doubtful order, and one of them was explaining to the other in utter seriousness: "This is the parking place for the lorries; this is the place where they load, and this is the place where they unload." He pointed with his finger at the different areas, which to me, of course, were all alike in the dust and the stones, but for him and his friend were unmistakably different and so it would be absurd for him to mistake the loading place for the unloading one. And the lorries went in and out, pieces of brick dragged and pushed by the children in turn, loading and unloading without a hitch, always going in at the entrance gate and out at the invisibly marked exiting gate. They had built their first factory, and it was a success. They had created a fantasy world in the midst of a dusty road. This is the precious faculty of my own playful child inside me: It can build a glittering palace in the dusty world I am living in. It can make me play with the bricks and stones of my daily job as though they were rubies and diamonds, it can make me see heavenly cities in crowded offices, and angels on the faces of men. I need my playful child in order to see my daily life through enchanted eyes.

The child has affection, tenderness, love. A child's hug around my stiffened neck is one of the most pleasurable feelings I know in life. It redeems with its warm innocence all the fear and guilt and loneliness of a suspicious mind. While a child is hanging on my neck, the world looks different and the air breathes clean. With a child I can be affectionate without misgivings, open without fear, loving without reservations. This is a rare blessing in a treacherous world. Once, during the time I was staying with Hindu families from house to house in my own city, I went to bed the first night and covered myself closely with the only blanket I had been given as it was an unusually cold night. As I was getting ready to sleep I heard dainty footsteps on the floor, a light shape trying to climb up my bed and get under my sheets, and the softened voice of the small boy in the house who was telling me: "Mummy has given you my blanket and I feel cold, and you will make room for me to sleep warm, won't you?" Of course I did. I slept soundly with the warmth of the blanket and the warmth of the child. I kissed him softly good morning when I got up and he was still asleep, tucked him up cozily against the morning cold, and went to face my day with the glow that a trusting and loving child had put in my heart. Let my own tenderness wake up within me to bring to the chill of life the warmth of the affectionate child.

A child is mischievous, and mischief is one of the most valuable ingredients of life on this planet. The surprise, the prank, the outburst of laughter. Taking life as lightly as it can be taken; being ready to laugh at oneself and ready to make others laugh at themselves, which everybody wants to do and nobody dares in the stiff formal society in which we move. It is all so ridiculous around us that the only sane thing to do is to poke fun at it and laugh at the ongoing, lifelong carnival we are staging. I fully identify with Natasha in Tolstoy's *War and Peace* when, on arrival in the city from her healthy life in the countryside, she is taken to an opera, sees the funny dress of those wealthy aristocratic men and women, their artificial gestures and high-pitched voices, looks around to check whether all feel what she feels and finds only polite bows and feigned admiration—and then suddenly feels the urge to jump onto the stage and start mimicking the actors, or to strike a nobleman with the fan in her hand or start tickling the woman by her side. She does none of that, of course, but her childlike nature is bursting within her to break through convention and jump into life. I have similar irrepressible thoughts and feelings when I am watching or even taking part in some solemn ceremony with formal dress and time-honored rubrics, and all look very serious and dignified, and I feel like jumping into the middle, dancing a jig, pulling a few people's hair, taking a deep bow, and passing around my hat for a collection. Outwardly, of course, I look as serious and dignified as anybody else, but at least I enjoy the circus in my mind.

In another family I was staying with during my house-to-house pilgrimage, a boy took the liberty of playing a trick on me. Daily I went to college on my bicycle, and cycled back in the evening to wherever I was staying, this being the most convenient means of transportation in the crowded, narrow, traffic-infested and cow-blessed streets of my beloved city. But that morning, as I went to take my bicycle from the front of the house where I had parked it for the night, it was not there. My heart missed a beat. Bicycle thefts are not a rare occurrence, and if mine had disappeared I would be put to a severe inconvenience in more than one way. I was looking around in despondency when the sound of a bell behind me made me turn sharply. There was my bicycle, and holding it and ringing its bell was the boy who had hidden it to see how the big man would react to a simple joke. To be honest, I was angry, but his face was so full of cheer, of laughter, of satisfaction at having fooled me that soon I reacted and valued more the sharing of the joke than the temporary fright at the imagined loss. I reflected: Many people appreciate me, look after me, honor me; but few have the courage and the confidence to fool me, and this fooling me can show greater closeness than all the praises and reverences in the world. I conveyed my

feeling to the child, who felt proud of his adventure. And I feel
happy to record it here.

I shall relate here a story of another child in another home.
Important to me as he made me recover, for at least one day, my
own sense of childhood. In the small room that was kitchen and
dining room and living room all in one I was sitting in a corner
on the floor doing my writing while the boy's mother was cooking the morning meal. I saw the child approach her and say
something that I did not hear but that obviously referred to me,
as both looked toward me during the brief dialogue. The child
had injured his foot and could not walk that day. There was no
bicycle in the house nor was there any other means of convey-
ance, as all in the family walked to their jobs; and so it was clear
that since the child could not walk he could not go to school,
and he felt badly about it as he was a good student who did not
want to miss class. What to do then? That was the point of the
little dialogue between mother and son in a hushed voice while
looking at me. The mystery of their look was soon explained.
The child walked shyly toward me and bent to be level with me.
I looked up, placed my hand on his head, and he spoke: "I
cannot walk today. Will you take me on your cycle and drop me
at my school on your way to your college today?" I felt a wave of
tenderness sweep through me when I heard his words and
looked at his face. He had trusted me. He had thought of me. He
had ventured to ask me to do what I never had done in my life:
take a child to school on my bicycle. I would not fail him. "Of
course we'll go together! Won't it be fun! Get ready, and as soon
as mummy feeds us we'll start. Only let me check my cycle,
because it never has had such a responsibility as today."

We started out together. I sat him on the handle bar and
cradled him with my arms as they bent around him to hold the
handles. I pedaled slowly and steadily, aware in every cell of my
limbs of the precious load I was carrying. For one day I had a
child to cycle to school; a borrowed child for a special day;

choice blessing for a celibate soul. I felt the perfume of his thick black hair against my face, the weight of his body in the extra pull my legs had to exert, the hanging stiffness of his injured foot, the music of his voice as he spoke from his vantage seat, the joy with which he rang the bicycle bell which I had entrusted to his care. We crossed the paths of other people carrying children on bicycles or scooters, real parents under the daily burden of the repeated trip. For them it was a routine chore; for me it was a rare privilege.

We reached the school, which I would have preferred were a longer way off. Other children were arriving on bicycles or by foot, some driven in motorcars, and the lively procession converged on the gate of the school where a teacher performed his daily job of welcoming the children. He saw me and recognized me. He knew who I was, and was understandably surprised to see me bring a boy to school. He watched me while I let my charge gently down from the bicycle, entrusted him to a classmate and reminded him of the exact time I would be at the gate to fetch him that evening. When I was getting back on my bicycle to continue my way, his curiosity got the best of that good teacher and he finally asked me the question that had been on his mind all the time: "Who was that boy?" "My child," I answered with joyful spontaneity, and drove contentedly away. I also was learning to play my own mischief.

33

The Spontaneous Child

The great virtue of the child is spontaneity. It does, on occasion, bring embarrassment to his parents in the presence of formal guests; but the balance of joy, freshness, and sheer enjoyment of life it brings to those who are privileged to live near a child is such that it abundantly makes up for the stray incidents in which a child's unchecked truthfulness brings a touch of color to the cheeks of adults around him. Indeed, even those passing blushings are later, when the guests are gone, a source of amusement when the incidents are described among friends in praise of the bold child. Do you know what he said? We all had trouble keeping back our laughter when he said it, but how right was he, wasn't he? Clever of him!

Blessed child who can say without flinching what he first thinks and who can describe the way he feels without censorship of mind or etiquette, irrespective of the tutored reactions in grown-up people. And blessed are those grown-up people when they can bring back into their lives the original playfulness of their early years, and combine in happy blend their mature wisdom with a spirited spontaneity. It is a difficult virtue to let ourselves feel what we really feel, and venture to express it good-humoredly before people who need a whiff of fresh air in their lives as much as we ourselves do. We are self-conscious, custom-ridden, stiff-necked. We lost our original innocence in the early breeze of an open paradise, and have trod along ever since through marked paths in dusty landscapes of established usage and accepted convention. When we realize the loss of our precious treasure we may begin to feel in ourselves the desire to recover it. This is a good sign that we are coming alive.

Here is the story of one such innocence lost. There is a famous statue I have admired since childhood and have seen reproduced in countless contexts, in gardens and museums, in photographs and reproductions; and I still contemplate it in the garden of a close neighbor on the lawn among creepers that enhance the grace of its classical pose. It is the statue of a young man with an innocent body, standing on one leg and removing from the other foot a thorn that had lodged itself in his flesh. The graceful balance, the supple body, the gentle curves, the effortless convergence of the youth's every trait on his sore foot in the expected instant of bodily relief . . . all make for an exquisite beauty and an artistic freshness that give pleasure to the eye and the soul of the sensitive observer. It is of this statue that the story is told, and the story-teller is Heinrich von Kleist, or rather an anonymous friend who told it to him.

That friend was one day bathing with a young man whom he describes as beautiful in body and innocent in mind, and, in their oblivious sport it so happened that the youth, standing on dry ground, took his foot into his hand and assumed, inadvertently, the pose of the young man in the statue. The same spontaneous stand, the same careless elegance, the same artistic obedience of all members of the body to the single focus of the raised foot. He then caught his reflection in a large mirror at the other end of the pool in the garden, was struck at once by the similitude and told the other man about his discovery. This other man, the friend in question, who was older and wiser, had also noticed by himself the striking parallel between the living youth and the stone statue; but, not to fan the youth's vanity, he had refrained from speaking of it, and even now when the young man mentioned the fact, the older man discounted it, denied any similitude and told his younger friend that he was seeing visions. The young man blushed and insisted, "Look, I'll show you. I'll do it again." He tried—but in vain. He himself realized that his pose was artificial, forced, ridiculous. He tried a second and third time, each time with worse results. He was tense, unnatural, worked-up. He must have tried about ten times, says the witness, but he never succeeded. He was nervous, ill at ease, angry with himself. He could never, for all his efforts, duplicate that first stand that had flowered by itself in unrehearsed beauty.

There is more to that incident. The friend in this story went on to say that from that day on, that young man was changed. He lost his charm, began to claim attention, grew self-conscious in the presence of women, and his gestures became stiff and his manners pretentious. "After a year had passed," he declared, "there remained not a trace of that loveliness that had so delighted everyone." The young man had literally lost his innocence. No efforts can recapture something whose essence is in its happening without effort. No training can recover the state that precedes all training. The young man who emulated the beauty of the statue will lose his own. The gates of paradise are closed.

Not entirely, though. The consciousness of what we have lost, the prizing of our former pristine innocence, the humility, openness, simplicity that go with a gentle desire and a constant readiness to regain what has been lost, can prepare the way for a new childhood—or at least for redeeming glimpses of it in the midst of our adult sophistication. We all have experienced in our lives those moments of lucidity when heaven opens, life looks transparent, the world makes sense, and a smile tells us that happiness exists. There are moments when we are truly ourselves, when the grace of spontaneity descends upon us and we find ourselves at peace with ourselves and with all around, aware of the blessing of truth in the kingdom of lies. The practice of living in the present, the contact with reality, the determination to be ourselves, can multiply those moments and bring relief into a drab world. Our best moments are our moments of true spontaneity, when we trust ourselves and all creatures around us and give without reservation what we have in us.

This happens in the arts. The best work of the Spanish composer Granados is the Intermezzo of *Goyescas,* and the way he composed it explains its inspiration. He had composed a two-act musical score for the stage, the piece had been rehearsed, the performance announced and the tickets sold when he was informed that there would have to be an orchestral interlude between the two acts. There was no time. If the individual scores had to be copied, and the piece practiced at least once, he had to produce it instantly. He did. The unavoidable urgency lent wings to his creativity: He sat down, forgot all constraints, gave free rein to the musical ideas in his mind, worked without interruption, and at one sitting completed what would be his life's masterpiece. If he had had a longer time to work on it, it would surely not have been so inspired. He literally forgot himself . . . and found his music.

The same thing is said about the Allegretto of Beethoven's Eighth Symphony. There are, it is true, sketches of its theme in previous papers, as Beethoven always kept notes of the musical ideas that came to him, but the writing of the whole movement seems to have been done at one sitting, and that would explain its unearthly perfection. The notes flow, play, dance so mischievously on the strings and the wood and the brass and the wind that they seem to be doing the whole job by themselves, while composer, players, and listeners have only to relax and enjoy the show. The difficult spontaneity that is the mark of genius.

Adam and Eve did us a bad turn on that fateful evening. They invited shame, grew self-conscious, and invented fashion. They made it hard for human beings ever since to be themselves in trustful simplicity. The coverings of the body are symbolic of the coverings of the mind—the deceits, the dissemblings, the false courtesy, the artificial manners. The false smile and the sweet meaningless words. The social mask. Dreary inventions of the adult world.

Unless you become like children, you shall not enter the Kingdom of God.

34

A Thousand Gurus

When an Indian saint was once asked who his guru was—a traditional question in a land where the belief that "without guru there is no salvation" is accepted dogma—he gave the names of several animals in nature, and explained with a smile that from them he had learned poise of body, spontaneity in action, and integration of behavior. Animals, not possessing a human mind, are unmolested by past guilt and future worries, and feel free in consequence to devote themselves fully to what they are doing at any given moment with a single unity of limb and sight. In that sense they are our gurus. They live in the present, clearly innocent of their total elegance. Walking lessons in nature's open school.

The cat is sleeping in a corner of the room. Watch its perfect sleep. The soft body folded on itself in furry laziness. The rhythmical heaving of the whole frame in contented slumber. The total ease. The supreme peace. The world does not exist for the sleeping cat, or rather has so fully blended with it that the cat is swept along in its orbit and lives in its air carried through life as the planet through the cosmos. Simply looking at the sleeping cat causes the tensions in my body to relax and dissolve as my eyes follow its curves, my ears get attuned to its breathing, and my whole being takes in the living image of untroubled rest. A cat does not need sleeping pills to achieve sleep in a troubled night. It does not have to perform relaxation exercises before going to bed to lure the hard-to-please goddess of sleep into its body. It has only to let itself be and close its eyes when they want to close. Sleep is at hand.

And then see how it wakes up. A noise, a scratch, a gust of wind, or something in its system has alerted its mind, and its whole body has responded with sudden alertness. Fully asleep when sleeping, and fully awake when awakened. With a knowing look it takes charge of the world around it and stands leisurely on its four legs. Then comes one of the most precious moments in the life of a cat and a privileged spectacle for the person who is fortunate to watch it unseen: The cat yawns and stretches itself with all its might, leaning on its hind legs and lengthening out its entire body right up to the front paws while its mouth opens wide to seemingly impossible limits for a tantalizingly long time. Every cell in its body opens up to fresh air and new blood. The body tests its suppleness and readies its responses. The cat stretches and stretches with a cheeky display of obvious pleasure. Watch and be jealous, human beings who are taught to stifle yawns and refrain from stretching! It is not polite. But it is healthy and pleasurable and great. The wisdom of letting the body find itself in the toning of its muscles and the filling of its lungs. The primeval ritual. The elementary yoga. Nature's morning prayer before a new day. The cat knows it well and gets the most out of the precious yawning after each sleep.

The cat plays and hunts. There is the story (apocryphal but amusing as are all music stories) of Chopin's fast Waltz in D Flat Major, composed while he watched a kitten play with a ball of woolen thread, pulling it out and getting more and more entangled in it till the kitten itself looked like a ball of wool, all covered with it and tied up in it. The legato notes in quick succession describe the playful running, the increasing tangle, the final helplessness and the open laughter. Man's heart rejoices at the lively pranks of the impish kitten, contemplating wistfully in it the freedom and mischief he secretly wants for himself. The pianist's fingers emulate the kitten's movements in Darwinian kinship, echoes of the same urge within different bodies. The waltz speeds on to its breathtaking finale.

Now the cat grows tense. It has seen its prey. No, it has seen nothing yet, but its organic radar has warned it of the presence of a mouse in the vicinity. Its eyes, its nose, its skin, its whiskers have tuned to the invisible waves, and it knows and it waits. Every joint of its body is now commandeered for immediate action. Its whole body, following the instinct of its senses, is pointed toward the exact spot where the deadly rendezvous will take place any minute now. No meditator in any school of spirituality, no Zen master, and no contemplative monk has ever achieved such perfect concentration of mind and body on a single thought for such an indefinite time. The cat does. It is a motionless statue in live expectation. And then it jumps. The human eye can hardly see the lightning arc, the instant sweep, the silent fall on the unwary prey. The mouse lies frozen in the sharp grip of the cat's pointed claws. A meal for the day, and then rest again on a contented stomach. Life as it comes. Full at each moment. The practical wisdom of living day by day, minute by minute without timetable slavery. Redemption from the clock.

A standard expression has been coined to describe the walk of the cat on any walkable surface: feline grace. Each member conscious of the whole, each limb independent yet aware of its responsibility, a unity in motion with each part in freedom. Much the opposite of the military gait that afflicts most humans and burdens their joints with lifelong complaints. Cats do not suffer from arthritis.

Cats are said to have nine lives. A fall from a height that would crush a human does them no harm, and they walk away unconcerned whereas the person would need an ambulance or a coffin. As a mathematics student I had to work out in exact equations the secret of the cat's fall to safety. Something to do with its center of gravity, which, when the head is being spontaneously lowered and the legs gently folded, moves down, balances masses, and prepares a landing on cushioned feet and springlike legs without harm to life or limb. A man in a free fall would brace himself for impact, clench his teeth, tense his muscles, lose his natural balance . . . and land with a thud in a heap of broken bones. We have lost the instincts that can protect us in body and mind. Cats lead healthy lives.

I have mentioned the heights of Mount Abu, that memorable haunt of wild life in land and sky, and of humans like me who want to regain their animal balance in therapeutic communion with Mother Nature. *Mej-Shila* at the back of *Shantishikhar* is a high cliff where a table-shaped flat rock sits in deceptive ease over a sharp drop of hundreds of feet over the far-off plains. It is a favorite platform for kites to come and rest from their spiral flights over the receding horizon. There are scores of the lordly birds at any point in the sky, sailing the winds with the mastery of their open wings. And I love to watch them while lying flat on their rock, with my head hanging over the cliff, my eyes level with their flight, so close that I can count the feathers on their wings and catch the offended glimpse in their swift eyes as they look in anger at my intrusive presence. What am I doing on their rock? I am learning from them. I too want to ride the winds and sail through life. I want their peace and their poise. I want brotherhood in the skies with the masters of spontaneous flight.

Creatures of ease. Models of freedom. Images of tranquility. No movement, no effort, no noise. How do they do it? How can they rise so high without flapping a wing? How can they cross the skies without flexing a muscle? Here comes, close to my face, a soaring kite, its wings extended, its legs retracted, its tail flat in the wind, its agile neck turning swiftly now to the right now to the left to let its keen eyes survey the world under it with pinpoint accuracy. It rises visibly before my gaze while all its body floats motionless in the air. How has it done that? How does it defy gravity? How does it soar unaided? I know its secret. The bird is one with nature. The kite knows the winds and the currents and the rising hot air and the swirling gusts of tropical mist. It knows the timings and joins the movement. The outside feathers of its right wing bend ever so little, and the bird is on course. Trust the wind, and you will go up. Trust nature and you will soar. Turn a feather, and you master the skies.

To be one with the tides and the seasons, with the wind and the sea. To befriend our own senses that are our family contact with creation outside. To reown our body in earthly covenant with the mud it came from. To trust our instincts and follow our hunches. To let the winds of grace rule our flight without the drag of unbelief. To relax, to accept, to enjoy. To know that life is friendly and the universe is home to our body. To feel the unity of our members in the totality of creation. Then our wings expand and our life flows. The whole universe is under our gaze.

And then the fish. Life in the sea. Transparent awareness. Supple existence. Instant spontaneity in three dimensions. All of it with a single attention focused to all sides for protection from any attack and instant feeding on any chance food. The fish lives literally on its awareness. A failure in that, and it misses its food or loses its life. Immediate reaction is its first code of conduct, and its first rule of safety. A turn of the tail and it faces its victim, a twist of a fin and it is gone unharmed. The freedom to move and the coolness to float indefinitely at any depth in the limitless waters. The effortless grace of its sleek curvature. A unity of movement in weightless performance. An aquatic ballet of silent music. The dance of the eternal sea.

The Hindus call their gods fish-eyed. The eye that is always open, ever watchful, never asleep. The eye that sees in darkness and probes the depths. The round perfection of global vision. The way the gods see. The way men are meant to see if they open their eyes and clear their minds and look without prejudice and understand without fear. Constant watch along the currents of the spirit.

A psychiatrist reports on a colleague who heals his patients by having them watch a fishbowl for long periods of time at a stretch. The leisurely rounds of the unconcerned goldfish apparently help the tense person to unwind and relax and forget his troubles and find peace in the miniature nature before him. I only wonder whether the fish will not go mad at the constant sight of the tense human who is gazing at it on doctor's orders. Someone has made a study designed to measure the harm caused to domestic animals by their owners, whose tensions and neuroses often affect their pets. Time for some enterprising ecologist to take nervous owners of healthy pets to task and claim a compensation. The red ibis of Venezuela turns grey in captivity among humans. Who will give it back its color?

Dogs, cats, birds, and fish. Animals of all kinds on nature's friendly grounds. Partners in free living. Masters of instinct. Reminders of plain behavior in a sophisticated world. We owe an ecological debt to these earthly companions for the silent lesson of their healthy senses and unspoiled reactions. These smaller brethren help us to fashion our own lives with the closeness to nature they embody daily before our eyes. We learn from them how to be what we are without hankering to be something else. "How absurd it would be if the elephant, tired of walking the earth, wanted to fly, eat rabbits and lay eggs like an eagle. Leave this to the human: to try to be something he is not!" said Fritz Perls. We could learn from them to be what we are, utilizing our fullest possibilities to the utmost degree in a generous commitment to every turn of existence. Animal wisdom in human bodies.

With a thousand gurus to teach us every day with the joy of their art and the grace of their presence, how is it we are so slow to learn?

35

The Broken Sandal

The great enemies of "to be" are "to do" and "to have." Man is judged not by what he is but by what he does or has, by his activities or his possessions, by his achievements or his bank account. And the consequent temptation is for me to do and to acquire, to fret and to hoard, to impress the world with the things I do, with the material possessions I have in wealth and the mental possessions I have in concepts and in plans for self-improvement and schemes for the betterment of mankind. Then the rush to act and to possess, to show results and break records takes hold of me and crowds out my very person from my own life. I become so busy with doing and getting that I have no time to "be." If I want to be myself, I have to begin by "being."

When asked, Who are you? most people answer what they are doing. I am a doctor, a student, a clerk, a housewife. Who are you? I'm working in a bank. And even better: Who are you? I am retired. Retired from what? From life? So long as you are alive you exist in full right, but one's being has been so much identified with one's work that once the work is over, life seems to be over, and one is simply "retired." True, it is not easy to give an all-encompassing answer to the question, Who are you?, but without getting into philosophies it should be possible to identify oneself without a working label or an identity card. Those who know me should know me not by my works or even my ideas and much less my external achievements, but by my own personality. I had an old professor who could never remember the names of any of his students, but would tell us feelingly and truly, "I know you by your souls." He definitely knew us better than others who could recite the whole roll-call by heart.

A competitive society imposes on its members the obligation to prove themselves. Pitiful obligation and intolerable burden. "I have to prove myself"—the very expression, accustomed as we are to it, is repulsive to linguistically sensitive ears. To prove myself? To prove that I exist? That there is such a person as myself? To demonstrate on the blackboard with chalk and chalk-duster the theorem of my own existence? To quote at least in clever escape, "I think, therefore I exist," or to start moving and take refuge in the other quotation, "movement is proved by walking"? To prove myself I have to prove that I can do great things, pass examinations, get degrees, obtain promotions, produce wealth. That will be "proving myself," won't it? A gallant proof that is. Chesterton has condemned "the nine-times-accursed nonsense about Making Good that teaches men to identify being good with making money." There are linguistic traps that expose the weakness of our thinking and the unacceptability of our behavior. The person has to be liberated from the burden of "proving himself" and "making good" in order to be able to just *be* himself in full right and noble dignity.

"I have done nothing in my life," I heard a grand old man say despondently. He had lived among giants who had performed wonders in pioneering fields, while he had spent his life in lackluster administrative jobs with no glamour and no publicity. In his life he had touched many hearts and lightened many lives with his cheerful nature and deep faith, but those good works had not been recorded in the annals of heroic deeds, and his name was not written in the chronicles of the history of his times. He had done nothing worth being counted, therefore he was nobody. Nothing to show, and therefore nowhere to be.

And yet as a man he was a great person who, with fidelity and self-effacement, had helped to run important institutions in difficult times. He fell a victim to the universal fallacy that equates a person's worth with his more visible doings, and put himself down in sad self-deprecation.

Shri Nisargadatta Maharaj, a truly enlightened soul of modern India, had a small tobacco shop in a crowded Bombay suburb, and that is all he "did" by way of business or profession if one has to judge by externals. Yet he "was" a great saint, and the collection of his enlightening conversations bears the meaningful title "I Am." A quotation: "I do not worry about the future. The right reaction to each situation is ready inside me if I trust my nature. I do not stop to think what it is I have to do; I just get started and act as it comes. Results do not affect me. I do not care whether they are good or bad. Whatever they are, they are. If they are adverse, I take them again in hand. In my actions there is no feeling of going towards a goal. Things happen as they happen; it is not that I make them happen, but that they happen as a result of what I am."*

To revalue the "I am" against the "I do" or "I have," a healthy detachment is useful. I keep on working as before, and do whatever is expected of me in my job and in my home, but I do not depend on results or possessions to measure the extent of my success in life. I can use things when they come my way, and can do without them when they are not available to me. Having an inner freedom from outside attachments, freedom to use them and freedom to do without—this attitude makes it much easier to go through life with peace of soul and the openness of mind to take what comes and to leave what goes. That enhances the person and revalues life.

Once I watched a beautiful scene—all the more touching as it was totally unexpected—that brought out before my grateful

* Sri Nisargadatta Maharaj, *Yo Soy*, Editorial Sirio, p. 138.

eyes, in image and parable, the lesson of inner freedom in the daily vicissitudes of life. I had gone for my daily walk in the early morning along the university grounds near our own house. A good many people, worshipers of clean air, were walking, running, or jogging along the many ways and spacious lawns of the large campus. Some, too, were on the way to their jobs at that early hour, servants of the morning in a labor-needy society. This must have been true of the little woman who was walking at some distance in front of me with small even steps and in a straight direction, likely toward the bus stop in her need to travel quickly to a distant workplace. I noticed her humble gait, her simple clothes, her steady progress on the road. She was certainly not there for voluntary exercise but for daily duty. She kept moving steadily toward her destination, and then suddenly she stopped. She bent and took her right sandal in her hand, the cheap rubber sandal with two straps worn over bare feet by most people in India. She examined it and tried to fix it. A strap had broken, and the sandal would not hold. An annoying accident on the way to work at the beginning of the day. Bad luck. What would she do? I watched. She quietly made sure that the sandal could serve no purpose any more, and gently she put it down on a side of the road. Then she removed her other sandal, rendered useless too by the failure of its companion, and laid it carefully by the side of the first, parallel relics of a morning letdown on the open road. Then she bowed lightly as though taking leave of the discarded footwear, and went her way barefoot in the same direction and at the same pace.

I watched and I reflected. If that accident had happened to me, or to many people I know, I would have felt annoyed, lost my temper, cursed the man who had sold me the sandal, thrown it away violently and limped back home, angry with myself and with creation at large. It is unfair to be left at the mercy of a stony road in the early morning: an inauspicious start of a day. I would have been upset and I would have felt bad. Not so that little woman, to all appearance. She had been unruffled, composed, resigned. She did not make a hasty movement or utter a loud word. She just saw the situation, examined it, reacted in peace. When she had the sandals, she walked with them; when she lost them, she walked barefoot. Ready to use them when she had them, and to do without them when she had them no more. She could walk alike with sandals and without them. A gesture of freedom. A lesson in acceptance. Take it when you have it, and leave it when it goes. The woman might not have known the Biblical words, but she acted them out: The Lord gave and the Lord took away; blessed be his name for ever. That was the object lesson of those two sandals, parallel at the side of the road in the morning dust. I approached the spot when the woman was no longer in sight. I remained for a moment looking at the sandals and thinking of the scene I had just witnessed. Then I too bowed to the sandals as the woman had done, and went my way. The morning walk had yielded its fruit that day.

36

The Golden Age

When I write here about living in the present I refer to this
actual moment that is to be lived in all its blessed intensity once
it is freed from the burden of past and future and can be appreciated for its unique intrinsic worth. Now, for the space of this
one chapter, I enlarge the meaning of "present" to mean the
present time, the times we are living in, the present of mankind
at this stage in its long history—as set against past times and
future times, much as the present time of an individual's life was
set against his or her past and future. And the phenomenon is
the same. Just as the individual person misses the present by
hankering for the past and fearing the future, so society at large
misses its appointment with the present by looking back nostal-
gically to the past or dreaming in escape or apprehension about
the future. If I am to live in the present time, I may do well to
reconcile myself to making the best of it as it is, not as other
times have been or as future times could be. This is common
sense. Yet this is not the common stand.

According to Hindu mythology we are living in the worst of
ages: *Kaliyuga*, the dark age when man's life on earth is short-
ened and his physical stature diminished, when truth dwindles
and virtue is scarce while vice is rampant and quickly working its
way to the cosmic destruction of the human stage, in order to
start creation's cycle anew with the clean dawn of a new *Satyuga*,

the Age of Truth or of Pure Being *(Sat)*. Not a very complimentary view of things as we know them. The past was great, in this view, whereas the present is miserable. Golden ages are all past; present, modern, postmodern times are the worst in mankind's history. Such historical pessimism darkens our perception of our own age. And we are the losers.

It is time we put in a good word for our misunderstood and disparaged age. It is true that much of what we have prized and treasured is gone, and its loss weighs heavily on our nostalgic memories. The times when things were clear and values definite, when white was white and black was black and everybody knew it and acted accordingly, praising good and condemning evil; when violence was not a daily word and the masked faces of international terrorism did not haunt our fair cities or threaten our fluttering hearts. Times of relative peace and general contentment, of stable prices and financial security, of firm principles and public faith. All that is gone, to a large degree, and in its place have come insecurity and inflation, doctrinal doubts and moral uncertainty, bombs in our streets and scandal in our hearts. And this change has taken place in our lifetime, before our eyes and in the brief span of a few years. We ourselves had known the old stability, not by hearsay but by experience, and we now find ourselves literally thrown into a turmoil we never expected and were not ready for. Everything has been shaken, and we stand in the middle of the imposing ruins not knowing what to do or where to go. We are bewildered by our own age; and when they tell us, not without reason, that its catastrophes are of our own making, that we are the causes (perhaps unwittingly) of the global crisis, we feel even worse.

There is much truth in this—and yet, with the proper perspective, each age is as good as any other, and the present one has its rightful, honored place in the ranks of history. Much has gone, yes, but well gone if it had to go. Old standards have gone, but new challenges have come. Uncertainty is no worse than certainty, and risk can be better than security. Unless we weigh anchor, the ship will not sail. Unless we let old structures drop we cannot build new ones, and—what may be more important and interesting—we would have no chance to learn to live without structures, at least without so many structures as we had before. We do well to let drop whatever wants to be dropped, to let things and events follow their course, so that ways and paths are cleared and room is made for new structures, new ideas, and new life.

The theologian Bernard Häring addressed to the Lord an inspired prayer, at the same time fully traditional and fully modern: "We praise you, Lord of the Church and Redeemer of the world, for being privileged to live in this great and difficult age. We thank you for the earthquake that has jolted us out of our drowsiness; you have driven away our self-complacency and tolerance of mediocrity. We thank you for the growing pains and tensions, for the new and never before dreamed-of opportunities of giving witness to you, the living God and Brother of all men. Lord, make us firm and joyful in faith, hope and love of God and of neighbor. Grant that we may read correctly the signs of this time of salvation and grow in maturity and openness. Give us the fortitude and wisdom to bear the risks of the full Christian life. When we make mistakes—and being human, we shall— help us to correct them with peace of mind and a sense of humor. Help us to outdo each other in mutual respect and charity and to bear each other in patience and good cheer. Lord, teach us how to pray and to transform life into prayer, into a colloquy with you. Teach us that holy worldliness which brings life and religion together and praises you, our Creator and Redeemer. Renew our hearts and minds, our passions and affections, that we may be able to fulfill our role in the renewal of the Church and society."

Bishop John A. T. Robinson applies to belief and behavior the expression used in the physical sciences about "the end of the stable state," and says with humble conviction: "I believe the crucial divide in the Church today is between those who basically accept (and even welcome) the end of the stable state (however painful) and those who deny or resist it. I am one of those who, with fear and trembling, welcome the end of the stable state." And then he quotes these words, full of faith, of Monica Furlong: "The best thing about being a Christian at the moment is that organized religion has collapsed. I cannot imagine a more enjoyable time to be a Christian, except possibly in the first centuries of the Church. For while the great holocaust is sweeping away much that is beautiful and all that is safe and comfortable and unquestioned, it is relieving us of mounds of Christian bric-a-brac as well, and the liberation is unspeakable. Stripped of our nonsense we may almost be like the early Christians painting their primitive symbols on the walls of the catacombs—the fish, the grapes, the loaves of bread, the cross, the monogram of Christ—confident that in having done so they had described the necessities of life."

The air smells again of catacombs and martyrdom, the people of God are again a minority, baptismal faith cannot be taken for granted, and to make the sign of the cross is an adventure. What can be more refreshing for the believing heart, more uplifting, more exciting? Gone is the safe routine of the past when each day was as the previous one, each situation was foreseen and each answer learned before the question arose. It was a fine age in its own way, as ours is fine and great in its way if we have eyes to see and courage to accept. The speed of life has increased, communication is instantaneous, problems multiply before answers can be found, and nobody can predict what comes next. This very challenge increases the human response, the vital energy, the capacity to cope with life in all its unexpected variety and growing insecurity. We are called to live deeper lives precisely because we are given more options.

To love our age, to be proud to belong to it, to feel at home in it is a great secret of inner peace and genuine satisfaction. To love our planet as it is, with its storms and earthquakes, its heat and cold, its lands and seas. To love our environment in field and forest, in deserts and mountains, in clouds and sun. To love our cities, maligned victims of modern civilization, condemned to be cursed by the very people who have built them and live in them. How can we be happy if we speak ill of our own homes, deride our environment, and accuse the air we breathe? Let us by all means fight to clean our streets, quiet our traffic, protect our seas, and purify our atmosphere; but at the same time let us enjoy what we have while we work to better it, while we plan for what it will become. Let us not despise the air we breathe today simply because we want to have cleaner air tomorrow. How can I be at peace with myself if I despise and insult the very air I am taking breath by breath into my lungs to support my life? How can I have love in my heart if I hate the air I breathe? How can I hold my soul in peace if I loathe the sounds I hear, the streets I walk, the buildings I live in? There must be no hate anymore in my heart for man or creature, wind or rain, dust or din. I love the city and the land, the smells and sounds, the sights of nature and men. I love, above all, the air I breathe, independent of its chemical composition which I leave to the experts to determine and to thoughtful humanity to improve. I love all that comes in to me; I accept my environment as it is, I protect my senses as best I can and then I let them free in a world of sounds and smells and taste; and I strive to enjoy what my senses bring to me from this world that is imperfect to be sure but full also of color and life. The desire to improve the future must not rob me of the capacity to enjoy the present, neither in my own life as a private individual nor in my cosmic responsibility as an inhabitant of this planet. We live in a wonderful time in a wonderful place, and the sensitive enjoyment of our presence in it is the best way to appreciate the true values of life and cosmos, and bring them out in our private lives, our social dealings, and our ecological behavior.

If we are in the worst of ages (*Kaliyuga*), a wise Indian sage also advises us that "for the enlightened man every instant is *Satyuga* (the golden age)." I notice the word "instant" in his saying. It is always the present moment that overcomes all obstacles, neutralizes all curses, and converts all doubts and fears into the joyful happiness of a life taken as it is. Heartfelt reconciliation with the present, in life, society, and history, is forever the way to peace and joy.

37

The Sacrament of the Present Moment

To live in the present is not so easy as it looks. Paradoxically, it takes a lifetime to learn the value of one day, a long training to learn how to concentrate on a passing instant—to master the difficult art of being fully where I am, yet ready at the same time to pass on fully to the next event when it arrives. Presence and departure. Commitment and detachment. The roots of an oak and the wings of a bird. Ready to stay and ready to fly as life moves on and creation follows its course. So easy to talk about. So hard to put into practice. Anyone who has tried knows what I mean.

When I was fifteen years old I heard a sermon in church that has remained in my memory ever since. The preacher described the impossible burden we all carry through our lives—the remorse and regrets about days gone by, and the fears and worries about the days to come—and then exhorted us with convincing eloquence to discover the "sacrament of the present moment," to entrust our past to the mercy of God and our future to his providence, and to live fully in the present without a care on our souls. I heard so many sermons in my youth, and all are now forgotten. But this one must have struck a special chord in me, because its pointed lesson never left me.

It all was so clear and so easy. There I had, at the beginning of my responsible life, a short formula, a providential guidance to direct my enthusiasm in the ways of the spirit with concrete advice and a sure rule. Live the present. The way to health and to faith, the kindly secret, the sure direction. My youthful mind grasped the idea with radical decisiveness, and my happy impatience saw itself carrying out the simple program in flawless efficiency for studies and prayer, for outlook and character. I felt lucky to have received so early in life the formula for salvation that would transform my life from that moment. I knew it. I would do it.

Yes, the idea remained. Remained where it was, high up in my head. It never really got down to the fields of actual practice. The years went by, and past and future rode on my mind as willful tyrants that scattered my efforts and tore the tissues of my spirit along all the directions of unstable thought. A beautiful sermon had become a nostalgic memory in my life. The idea still beckoned to me, but its practice escaped all my repeated efforts and willful resolutions. It was not easy to live in the present.

Time passed, and the opportunity came for me too to give sermons and write books. I was ready to pass on to others the beneficent formula . . . without having mastered it myself. In the first book I published in the Gujarati language in India, a book of guidance for youth as I had received it at their age, I included a full chapter on "the sacrament of the present moment"; this was written with clarity and conviction, as the idea had been with me for so many years by then. More than one young reader told me that the chapter had been particularly enlightening for him, and that in it he had found the key to a happy and healthy life and he needed no more. I nodded my blessing. They were right as I had been. They would find out as I had found out. Let the seeds grow anyway. Some good is always done, and some plants take long to grow.

More years passed, and now I have sat down to write, and

almost completed, a whole book on that key theme: Live the present. I try to live the present in freedom from fears and conditionings as the true way to be myself day by day in renewed creation. The discipline of writing to activate my own resources of being. The haunting idea expressed in new ways through story and experience, through longing and contemplating, through love and faith. There it is before me, clear as the pole star in an open night, perfect as a theorem in one of Euclid's books. The naked perfection of life on earth. So simple and so distant. The tantalizing seduction, the never-ending quest.

Is there any method? Krishnamurti spent his life answering people who asked that question: "Sir, there is no method," was his repeated answer. Euclid told King Ptolemy who had asked him to teach him geometry, but in a short way in consonance with his royal status: "Sir, there are no shortcuts to geometry." The things that have real value in life have no shortcuts to lead up to them. There is no magic formula, no quick remedy, no instant revelation. Straight is the way and narrow is the gate. If there were a short way, the goal would not be worthwhile. It is a long way and a dark night. There are the doubtful steps, the occasional setbacks, the recurring discouragement; the sudden hope, the glorious glimpse, the anticipated celebration; the new slope and the renewed effort, the easy confidence, the joy and the fear, the long patience in faith. Who can describe the path of the greatest adventure of man on earth? His determination to be himself, to find his face, to dare his fate; to seek his soul in the undaunted resolution that fires him with courage unto death and with faith beyond death right up to the other side of earthly life, into the very presence of the Father who created him in his image and likeness, and who alone can grant him the grace of the ultimate discovery of his own divine identity in the mirror of faith! There is no replacement for the personal commitment to sincerity and truth before the witness of angels in wonder.

Wasn't man placed just a little below them, almost touching them?

A few anecdotes now follow to lighten the tension of this passionate climax in the vital quest of ultimate identity.

After many years of obedient discipleship in discipline and service, the eager and frustrated disciple asked his master: "For more years than I can count I have served you with utmost fidelity, have done all you have told me and learned all that you have taught me; yet nothing has happened to me yet, and you have not discovered to me the secret of enlightenment. What are you waiting for?" The master answered: "I was waiting for you to ask that question." And he went on exactly as before.

An impatient inquirer could hold himself back no longer, obtained the address of a recognized master, broke into his house and asked peremptorily to be shown the way to self-realization. He was given the answer: "I have three things to tell you. First: You are at this moment so excited that you will not be able to understand any doctrine I may explain to you. Second: You are stepping on my toes. Third: You have come to the wrong person; the master you seek lives in the next house."

The British method to obtain a perfect lawn: Prepare the ground. Remove offending roots. Sow the seed. Spread manure. Then water regularly for six hundred years.

This last method comes closest to the attitude required for the greening of the self: Wait. Sow the seed and relax. Observe. Watch. Keep things in mind. Be alert and ever mindful. Keep in touch. Be there. Visit your lawn daily. Trust nature. Allow the rain. Let the sun play on the grass. So too can we describe the way to live the present, to be oneself and to find reality, to meet life, to welcome grace, to prepare the ways of the Lord—one must be ever watchful, with lamp in hand and feet on the ready, eyes on the horizon and heart over the clouds. One must be the wise virgin, the faithful servant, the loving friend.

To watch my own thoughts, to uncover the roots of my conditionings, the birth of my prejudices, the growth of my fears. To watch, to discover, to unearth, to bring to light all that happens in my inner darkness. To bring to the surface of my consciousness all that goes on in my uncensored subconscious. Just to know, to unmask, to make light. No resolutions, no self-imposed exercises, no moral violence. Nature is wise and grace is ready if only we open the way to them by seeing where we stand and realizing what we need. Therefore watch and observe. Day by day, hour by hour, around the clock that is life. The ever-watchful person is the one who will catch the first ray of the rising sun and will let the sunshine into his life with open gratitude. The one who learns how to watch himself will find himself.

The greatest adventures of man on earth have been discoveries. A new continent, a new summit, a new chemical element, a new star. There is a great discovery awaiting each one of us, daring in its boldness and rewarding in its prize: the discovery of our own selves. To find myself. To know myself. To be myself. Will man, the great discoverer, ever discover himself?

38

Rediscovering: A Parable

The child had gotten his toy. The one he wanted, in the latest fashion and at a high price. He had seen it advertised on TV, had asked, pleaded, coaxed, and cried till his mother capitulated and his father acquiesced and they went to the shop and bought the toy and he came back home hugging it possessively against his breast as a priceless treasure. He was told plainly that the toy was expensive and that the toy budget for the year had been spent on it and so no more toys could be expected in the coming months; and he understood the warning and accepted the condition because that was the toy he wanted, and if he had it he did not care to have any other. As soon as he got home he called his friends and showed them his new toy with pride and satisfaction. Wasn't it great?

Yes, it was. But the elation did not last long. After a few days one of his friends in the neighborhood also got a new toy and came to show it off, and it too was of the latest fashion and a still higher price, so that the first child's toy faded before it in comparison, and that was the end of its charm. The child lost his interest in it, and yesterday's treasure became today's rubbish.

His mother tried to explain to him that his own toy was a very good one, perhaps even better than that of the other boy, that it had cost a lot and there would be no more toys now for some time, so he had better take things as they were and play with his toy. But the child looked away, sulked, and showed displeasure, and the new toy, like a once-favorite queen now rejected, remained forgotten in a corner of the room.

The child's mother had her own problem too. She had a new home, having had her own house built after much saving and planning and working. She had made sure it would be modern and attractive in every way, an ideal building in an elegant neighborhood. There was also a small garden around the house, and she had planned every corner of it and nursed every plant with her personal care. When they went to live in the new house she invited friends and acquaintances to a party, showed them around the house and explained with detail and taste the thinking behind the structure, why this room was set in this style and why this window opened on this side. She took pride in her house and demonstrated this in her daily care of it. She was meticulous in keeping the house spotlessly clean, and tended the garden lovingly day by day.

This was till a new house was built in the neighborhood. Not much different, not much bigger, not much newer, but perhaps a little more modern, a little more daring. When it was completed the new neighbors invited her to the housewarming, and the gracious hostess took her around the house and explained with love and insight the planning of each corner and the setting of each window. And our woman saw it all and listened and nodded and showed appreciation, but when she went back to her own house she looked at it anew and her heart fell. The house looked inferior and commonplace, not worth any attention or any special care. From that moment she lost interest in her own home, and her loss of interest showed in her loss of care for the house and the garden. She stopped taking the trouble to keep things clean and beautiful, so that dirt accumulated in the corners of the house and weeds grew unchecked in the lawn.

Her husband noticed the change in the home atmosphere and the change in his wife; gently he inquired about the cause and eventually found out. His wife was no longer interested in their house because the neighbors' house was better. He then tried lovingly to explain to her that their own house was fine, even better in some respects than that of the neighbors; that it had cost a lot, and that they had to live in it now anyhow because the budget for new houses had been used up and no new house could be expected, so they had better take things as they were and make the best of their house and their garden and lawn. But the woman remained silent, sulked, shrugged her shoulders—and yes, she continued to live in her house, but she did not take care of it anymore and allowed things to deteriorate. She did not give parties now or invite guests anymore, and when some came on their own she did not show them around the house, she did not explain the planning of each room or the setting of each window. And she no longer tended the garden herself.

And that woman's husband and that child's father had also his own personal delicate problem. He had gotten a wife, having married that woman a few years ago, and a fine woman in every way she was, with glamour and intelligence, affection and care. He was in love with her, appreciated her worth, and took her along to feasts and parties with joy and enthusiasm whenever he had a chance. He took pride in introducing her to his friends and in acknowledging their sincere compliments about her. He boasted of having a wonderful wife, and liked to proclaim happily while he held her hand, "We are the happiest couple on earth!"

That was till other friends got married and other couples were formed, and his friends introduced him to their young wives. Many of them were truly accomplished and attractive, some having special beauty and some great intelligence. And as he came to know them he noticed that his interest in his own wife dwindled and his affection for her diminished. There was nothing wrong with her, but she now seemed ordinary, uninteresting, dull. And his lack of appreciation began to be reflected in his behavior. His feelings toward his wife cooled down and his daily attentions to her diminished visibly. Serious domestic danger.

He did try to persuade himself that all this was wrong, that his wife was fine as she had always been; that in any case they had to live together for life and so he had better take things as they were, be reconciled with the facts, and bring back the lost affection and the vanishing interest before it was too late. But he did not succeed. A growing coldness crept between them, and yes, they continued to live together, they even went out together when they had to; but he did not take her out on his own, did not willingly take her to parties, did not introduce her to friends, and never again said that they were the happiest couple on earth.

A dullness of life had settled on a family of three. A child, a woman, a man. A toy, a home, a wife. First enthusiasm, then a test, finally disillusionment. Will that be the way of all flesh?

Then one day that child was alone in his room and his eyes fell on the old abandoned toy in a corner. He looked at it, recognized it, went closer to it. He made sure that nobody could see him, so as not to lose face before anybody in his moment of repentance—and then he took the toy in his hands, shook off its dust, saw that it was a fine toy well worth playing with, smiled happily to himself in silent reconciliation, and started playing with it contentedly. He had not noticed that the door of his room was open and his mother was watching him from the next room with loving curiosity and attentive expectation. She had understood the gesture, and respected the seriousness of the moment. She did not say a word, because she knew with a mother's instinct that if she spoke she would spoil everything. But she felt happy in her heart that her child had made friends again with the old toy, and she smiled to herself in silence.

On another day that woman was sitting alone in her home when she looked around her and suddenly realized how much dust had settled on the furniture, how the paint on doors and windows was peeling off, how the wallpaper was scratched in many places, and how wild and messy the garden was. How could that have happened? She rose at once, began dusting chairs, wiping tables, sweeping floors, and then went out into the garden and started putting order and taste into the flowers and plants. Her interest in her home and her garden had flowered all of a sudden within her, and she had become again the intelligent and efficient housewife she used to be. She was enthusiastically going about her chores when her husband returned from the office. He saw her from afar at work in the garden and he noticed the change. He at once understood what had happened, and rejoiced at its meaning. He did not say a word, as he was afraid that if he spoke he would wound her sensitivities and spoil the mood; but seeing his wife reconciled with the house and the garden, he felt very happy.

And on yet another day, late in the evening when husband and wife were seated in their room reading silently each in a chair, each in a mood, the husband looked at his wife and suddenly realized again what a wonderful woman she was and how much he had always loved her and still loved her all the more now, and wondered how he could have been so foolish as to allow such an estrangement without any cause for such a long time. And as they were alone in the room he rose slowly and deliberately, went toward her with glowing anticipation of pent-up pleasure, took her gently in his arms to soften the surprise, lifted her up with her willing and expectant cooperation, and brought her to himself; and they both renewed in blessed intimacy the sacred tryst of their first love. And God saw them. He saw them from afar without their noticing him. He did not want to distract them or make them self-conscious; but when he saw husband and wife reconciled at long last to each other, God felt very happy indeed.

A child rediscovers his toy, a woman her home, a husband his wife. When shall I discover, find, enjoy my own self?

39

Tell Me Who I Am

On a momentous day of his earthly existence Jesus faced his disciples, came close to them in confidence and intimacy as he had never done before, and asked them in tender mystery and sacred adventure: "Who do you say I am?" Jesus wanted to find himself reflected in the love and understanding of the people who for three years had been closest to him, had been by his side day and night, had listened to every word he said and had watched every action he performed. Jesus wanted to find in faith and affection the statement of his unique personality, to hear in human language the expression of his personal being, to find in friendly faces the divine traits of his own countenance. Jesus wanted the support for his "Who am I?" from the people who knew him best and loved him most.

With the same trust and deep need we too can seek Jesus' reaction to our search for identity and our striving to be ourselves. We too can approach him with genuine openness and deep reverence and ask him in the close friendship of intimate prayer: "Lord, who do you say I am?" You know me better than I do, you have made me and lived with me and know my past and my present, my desires and my fears, my ideals and my failings, my dreams and my realities. As you have made me I want to be myself in the fullest possible way, to bring your work to fruition and show your art in my clay. I want to be myself because you have made me, and my only way of giving you glory is to be with all my heart all that you intended me to be. I want to know what that is, I want to know myself, so that I can chisel every feature and bring out every color in your handicraft. Tell me, Lord, who I am in your sight that I may strive to be so in my life.

We know ourselves best in dialogue with God, in faith and commitment, in liturgy and prayer. Facing God who is ever present and ever new we recover our own presence and our own newness, and we learn from him—who in his infinite being never repeats himself—the permanent freshness of the eternal present.

Jesus himself reminded us of the value of the present before God and before man when he exhorted us to throw our worries on the providence of our heavenly Father, who knows what we need before we tell him, who looks after us even better than he looks after the flowers and the birds, who will provide for all our needs of soul and body with unfailing interest and loving care. "The day is enough to itself" is the basic formula for peace of mind which he proclaimed from the Mount. One step at a time. Today in its fullness. No yesterday and no tomorrow. Rid yourself of the conditionings of yesterday and the worries about tomorrow, and you will find peace, wholeness, and joy. Live the joy of each morning with the flowers and the birds, and you will know the joys of creation and the blessings of life. Live from moment to moment with the symphony of creation that sounds uninterrupted throughout heaven and earth. Enjoy each note as it flows in daily melody through the clouds of heaven and the moods of man. Let yourself be carried by the winds of grace and the currents of instinct. Be inspired by the spontaneous flight of the bird that knows no bounds because the universe belongs to its wings; by the ready opening of the flower in the morning perfume of a friendly earth. No care for the morrow because there is someone who knows and loves and cares, and so all will be well with each hour under his providence.

The people of Israel in their march through the desert—image and rehearsal of our own march through life—were fed by the Lord with the daily blessing of the timely manna. A peculiarity of the providential food was that it was to be collected daily, and if anyone, in the greed of hoarding provisions or the simple laziness of saving tomorrow's gathering by loading double today, took on one day the ration of two, this extra ration would rot and be filled with worms making it unfit for human consumption. The manna was thus strictly a daily food. Only on Fridays each person had to gather double to avoid working on the Sabbath, and the food then lasted the two days in good condition. Take only what you need today. Eat it happily and tomorrow will bring its own food. Each day for itself. Each hour on its own. Take your manna and keep walking, and tomorrow will bring its own share in the unfailing providence of the Lord who looks after his people on the sands of the desert and in the pilgrimage of life. "Give us today our daily bread."

When we live with this filial dependence on God's loving care, when we walk our path in life with Jesus on our side in daily faith and growing affection, when we approach as he did the maturity of our life in the quest for self-knowledge, we can turn again to him and ask the question of our life, of the secret of our being and the search for our own heart. In a moment of quiet intimacy, in the twilight of prayer, in the silence of contemplation, we ask the trembling question: "Lord, who do you say I am?" And then the miracle takes place that opens the heavens and releases the dove, and a voice resounds in the depths of our heart with the whole creation as witness and the waters of the Jordan washing away the unworthiness of our frail bodies: "You are my beloved son." Grace of adoption. Words of the Father. Sons in the Son. Divine charter of our humble existence.

Thank you, Lord. I want to be myself. I want to be your son. I want to be your beloved son.

About the Author

Carlos G. Valles, S.J., is a Spanish Jesuit priest who has worked in India for the past nearly forty years, and became a close friend and associate of the late Father Anthony de Mello, S.J. He has written dozens of books, for which he has received India's highest literary award as best prose writer. His most recent works include *Mastering Sadhana: On Retreat with Anthony de Mello* and *The Art of Choosing* (both published by Image Books/Doubleday).